MISSION IN BURMA

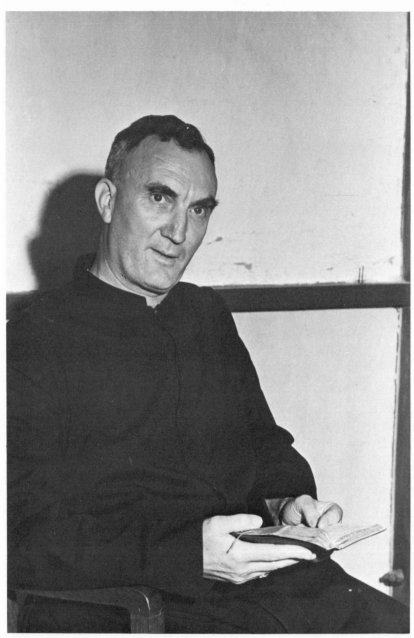

Monsignor Usher

MISSION IN BURMA

The Columban Fathers'
Forty-Three Years in Kachin Country

BY EDWARD FISCHER

У У У

A Crossroad Book · *The Seabury Press*

1980
The Seabury Press
815 Second Avenue
New York, N.Y. 10017

Design by Victoria Gomez

Library of Congress Cataloging in Publication Data

Fischer, Edward.   Mission in Burma.

1. Missions—Burma.   2. Missions to Kachin tribes.
3. St. Columban's Foreign Mission Society—History.
4. Catholic Church—Missions.   1. Title.
BV3270.F57   266'.2591   80-16897
ISBN 0-8164-0464-X

CONTENTS

MISSION IN BURMA

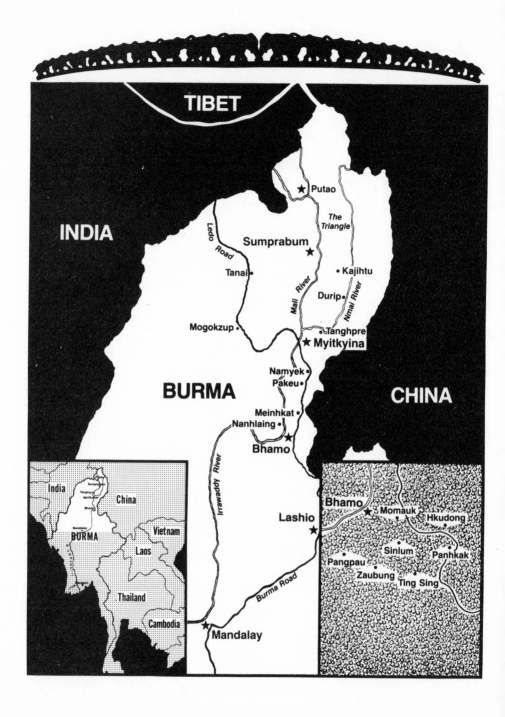

One

BEGINNINGS IN BURMA

"Green Hell" is what one of Merrill's Marauders called it when he
met a missionary along the trail. "Green" for the wild dense jungle that smothers hill after hill; "hell" for malaria, typhoid, and monsoons, to say nothing of tigers, elephants, and cobras.

"Home" is what the missionary called it for he had lived there nearly
a decade. Having arrived with the Columban Fathers in 1936, he
worked in the Kachin hills of upper Burma until war found its way into
that remote wilderness.

Rumors about Burma had been plentiful when the missionary and
twenty-five other young men were nearing ordination in Ireland. Word
went around among them that the Columbans would soon undertake
another mission in addition to those in China, Korea, and the Philippines.

After ordination, at Christmas of 1935, the new priests continued
studying at the seminary while awaiting their appointments. Months
passed and rumors intensified, until one morning in May the class
president, Father Thomas Murphy, moved among his friends in the
lecture hall. He placed a hand on each of five shoulders, saying, "You
are appointed to the new mission in Burma." He, too, would be with
them, he said.

The young men were pleased to hear that Father Patrick Usher
would also be going to Burma as their superior. At the seminary they
had come to admire the thirty-six-year-old Usher, a tall man with
quick, energetic movements, sharp features, and sandy hair as resil-
ient as wire.

Patrick Usher, born May 12, 1899, in the parish of Tullyallen, in
County Louth, had studied at St. Patrick's College, Armagh, before en-
tering the celebrated theological seminary at Maynooth, near Dublin.
At the end of his second year at Maynooth, Usher decided to join a

I

mission society that was only three years old. He transferred to the seminary at Dalgan Park, County Galway, where, even before his ordination in 1923, he was appointed business manager. A tame assignment it was for a man who enjoyed adventure.

Now, after thirteen years, Father Usher was destined for Burma. Immediately, his characteristic impatience came bubbling up. He had to be up and doing, getting things done. So he announced that he would sail in September, a month before the priests in his care.

The young priests had scattered across Ireland to enjoy the last holiday at home for ten years. All except the Australian, Bernard Way. Since he was just marking time at the seminary, he volunteered to accompany Father Usher.

The two Columbans sailed from Dublin for England and there boarded the S.S. *Mulbera* of the British India Line. After a month's voyage which brought them to Calcutta, they transferred to a ferry steamer for the rest of the way to Burma.

At dawn on October 21, 1936, the steamer stopped to pick up the harbor pilot in the wide, muddy expanse of sea where the Irrawaddy empties into the ocean. The boat churned yellow water cluttered with scum, flotsam, and water hyacinths. Gradually, Rangoon took form in the mist, its flatness and drabness relieved only by the golden, gleaming spire of the Shwe Dagon pagoda.

As the ferry steamer approached the dock, a man standing at the rail beside the missionaries said, "Look, that fellow forgot to take off his nightshirt!" He pointed to Father Patrick Donoghue who was standing there waiting in his white soutane.

In spite of his name, Father Donoghue was of dark complexion, for he had been born in Rangoon, the son of an Irish father and an Indian mother. He and Father Usher had become friends at the Columban seminary when Donoghue, a lay doctor, was en route to China as a medical missionary. In time he had studied for the priesthood in Penang and was ordained for the diocese of Rangoon where he remained.

Father Donoghue took the Columbans on a tour of the city, which at the time had a population of 400,000. They observed that Rangoon lacked the look of a Burmese city, for most of the population was alien: Indian, Chinese, European, and Eurasian. The Burmese, Father Donoghue explained, lived on the outskirts and on a few streets near the Shwe Dagon, so they were strangers in their own capital.

The visitors were surprised to see so many Buddhist monks, their saffron robes adding color to every street. And the pagodas, so many of them! The Columbans took delight in the tinkling of temple bells, the soft-toned echoes of gongs, and incense heavy in the air. Everything reminded them of Kipling.

When ready to start on the road to Mandalay, Father Donoghue put them aboard a narrow-gauge railroad, the first step of a 750-mile journey to Bhamo. The tiny engine chugged along for 18 hours across a flat, alluvial plain, one of the richest rice fields in the world.

The priests scarcely slept, they were so keyed up watching the exotic sights of the Far East: men riding teak logs down the Sittang . . . women pounding clothes on rocks in shallow streams . . . vendors passing rice and curry through the coach windows. On past Pegu, Toungoo, and Meiktila they looked and looked until their eyes ached.

At the station in Mandalay, an effervescent Frenchman and a more sedate Burman, both wearing white soutanes, greeted the Columbans. As the Frenchman rushed about searching for baggage, Father Usher asked the Burman where Bishop Albert Faliere might be. The Burman, Father Joseph U Win, nodded toward the Frenchman pulling trunks out of the railway carriage.

Bishop Faliere was forty-seven years old at the time, with a long black beard and an ample mustache, both with lots of bristle and crackle to match the glint in his eyes. He was a member of Missions Etrangers de Paris, the Foreign Mission Society of Paris. This was the second time the Columbans had been asked to cooperate with the French missionaries; two years earlier they had begun work in Korea under direction of the distinguished Bishop Demange. As far as Fathers Usher and Way were concerned the Foreign Mission Society of Paris was "the big league" in mission work. So many of its priests came out for life, while they, Columbans, were looking forward to a visit home in ten years.

The Columbans were touched by such anecdotes as the one about the old French missionary who served without going home in a remote part of Burma for fifty-seven years. When he heard that a confrere was on his way to Paris, he wrote: "When you return to France, call at my home and kiss for me the little Annette." He remembered his sister as she had been at age seven on the day of his ordination. When the priest returned to Burma, he did not have the heart to tell his compatriot that when he went to deliver the message, it was an old woman who raised her cheek to be kissed.

Right off the Columbans took a liking to Bishop Faliere. He was an excellent companion and a tour guide beyond compare. The Mandalay he showed them, unlike Rangoon, was truly Burmese. In the city of 150,000 people, the bishop said, about 10,000 were Buddhist monks, called *pongyees*. Don't expect too many conversions from among the Buddhists, he said in passing.

The bishop assured his guests that Christian missionaries were no longer dying violent deaths in Burma. He told of two French missionaries put to death by drowning at Pegu by order of the king. "That was in 1693," he hastened to add. And Bishop Gallizia was killed in the jungle near Pegu by the king's soldiers in 1745. Father Nerini was beheaded at Syriam in 1756 and his head was sent to the king. A native priest, Father Moses Nya U, died of torture in prison at Armarapoora in 1852.

And so ran the stories that could have been discouraging to men starting missions in Burma, except that exotic Mandalay made all seem right with the world. In those days, there was still a relaxed, easygoing charm in lower Burma. As a colonial Englishman said, "It was a land where it seemed always Saturday afternoon."

The bishop, a lively historian, told of the building of the city in such a way as to make it come alive. It had been begun as recently as 1858 by Mindon Min, the second last king of Burma. How near the bishop made it seem! The British warships sailing up the Irrawaddy in 1885, and the king and queen, Thebaw and Supaya Lat, being taken aboard a man-of-war to die in exile.

Their old palace felt haunted, deserted and lonely within its crenelated walls. The bridges and pagodas still gleamed white in the sunshine, but its golden mirrored halls had lost their lustre and the golden throne rooms were dusty and tarnished.

While never out of sight of Buddhist pagodas, Bishop Faliere was still able to show his guests an impressive Catholic side to Mandalay. They visited a technical institute for boys and several good schools and orphanages. At a leper asylum the Columbans little realized what an important part this asylum would play in their lives and in the lives of their colleagues still on the way.

The bishop was proud of the cathedral, a building financed by two Burmese Catholics. He showed his guests four other city parishes with good churches. His enthusiasm was muted when he spoke in a mood of discouragement about the neglected mission stations in the vast wilderness of northern Burma.

The Columbans knew that they had been asked to come to Burma because the bishop's own society was hindered in its work by a lack of missionaries. The war that had raged in Europe from August of 1914 until November of 1918 took the lives of so many young Frenchmen that now there was a shortage of priests.

When it came time to leave, the bishop insisted on accompanying Fathers Usher and Way on their four-day riverboat trip up the Irrawaddy to Bhamo. During the unhurried journey, with long stops at Twinnge, Meza, and Katha, the Columbans searched the shore for new sights and listened to the bishop tell of Burma and its people.

He pointed out how north of Mandalay the country turns into rocky bluffs covered with tangled jungle and tall elephant grass. The visitors were pleased by the picturesqueness of little villages rambling along the bank of the river with long flights of steps descending through dark green foliage to the water's edge.

Soon mountains moved in close to form the Irrawaddy defile. Above Katha, Father Usher observed, "Now the Irrawaddy looks more like a river and less like a series of lakes." The mountains came in exceedingly close to create the gateway to Kachin country, the land where the Columbans would work out their destiny.

Once more mountains receded until the landscape spread out, making way for open plains. The boat slowed down in the wide stream and swung completely around toward a crude jetty floating in the stream. Three French priests stood waiting on the low brown bank. The end of the journey: Bhamo.

Two

THE OTHERS ARRIVE

When Fathers Usher and Way left the seminary for the Far East the other young priests assigned to Burma were visiting their homes. James Stuart was in Derry, Daniel Cooney in Cork, Thomas Walsh in Waterford, Thomas Murphy in Kildare, and William Kehoe in Dublin. Another Columban added to the list, Denis McAlindon, of Lurgan, County Armagh, had been working toward a degree in theology at the Gregorian University in Rome ever since his ordination two years earlier.

The six gathered on Tilbury dock in London, October 10, 1936, to board the S.S. *Domala,* a slow freighter-passenger ship scheduled to reach Calcutta in six weeks, more or less. Once aboard, the young men were confronted for the first time with a now extinct species, "the British Raj." These were Englishmen who moved from station to station around the world doing their best to hold the Empire together.

The Raj looked upon missionaries, especially Irish missionaries, with some disdain. Life on shipboard, however, thaws attitudes, and before long the Irish and the English were playing games together on deck. The English must have found the young men attractive and amusing, even though a little mad. What puzzled the Colonial British was why missionaries should go to the Far East to work under harsh conditions when it was possible to find employment there in tea plantation management, railroad administration, the civil service, and the army. Why live like a native when you can sit on the club verandah in the cool of the evening watching polo and sipping gin?

The Englishmen asked questions that the young priests would hear time and again before their ministry was over: What is the meaning of life? Is there a God? What about contraception? As one of the missionaries recalled forty years later: "We dutifully drew on all the theoretical knowledge accumulated during the seminary years. And we were nonplussed at the lack of impact that even our most reasoned arguments had. To us they seemed obvious and compelling. So much for our first missionary efforts!"

The ship made long stops at Malta, Port Said, Aden, Columbo and Madras, all places with one thing in common: a great glare in the sunlight, a sight painful to eyes accustomed to mists and greenery. At Calcutta the Columbans said goodbye to the *Domala,* a ship destined for a grave in the English Channel when hit by German bombs in the Second World War.

It was in Calcutta that the Belgian Jesuit, Archbishop Perier, told the Columbans that he had a place for them in his diocese should events in Burma turn out not to their liking. This misled the young men into thinking that if the archbishop of Calcutta wanted them, the archbishop of Rangoon would receive them with delight.

Not so.

Four days later in Rangoon, Archbishop Provost, of the Foreign Mission Society of Paris, and his French priests treated the visitors in a way that caused one of them to recall many years later: "It had all the appearances of a snub, and I was not alone in my thinking." Fathers Usher and Way had had similar treatment a few weeks earlier. Father Way said long afterward, "In Rangoon they thought it a bit of a disgrace to have to call priests from another country and another nationality." Father Donoghue explained that Bishop Provost had nothing against the Columbans, but felt that French priests would in time be able to do the work they had come to do.

But Rangoon did not have the problem of upper Burma, and Mandalay did. That is why Bishop Faliere had written to Rome begging for assistance. When he heard help was on the way, he wrote to the superior general of the Columbans: "The news is most welcome. I want to tell you how glad we feel to know that the new missionaries, in great numbers we hope, are to come and help us. They will be very, very welcome." Later when someone suggested to him that perhaps the bishop of Rangoon did not approve of having the Columbans in northern Burma, he merely said, "Rangoon is not Burma."

In Rangoon a long letter from Father Usher awaited the young priests. It started by saying: "Our Bhamo, translated, means 'pot village.' The people who gave out the place names here were apparently in poor form the morning they came here. The name was not one of their best efforts. In the first place, ours is no village but a respectable town, and, in the second, it has nothing more to do with pots than any other town. The reason for the name is that we are situated in the middle of a plain surrounded on all sides by hills about twenty miles off. It may be admitted that there is a general resemblance to a great pot, but it need not have been advertised."

The new arrivals were puzzled by Father Usher's instructions: "First of all buy a bed." They pictured a substantial piece of furniture with four legs, headboard, footboard, springs, and mattress. Knowing their way of thinking, Father Usher advised them to ask Mother Ligouri, the superior of the Good Shepherd convent of St. John, to describe the kind of bed needed and to suggest where such might be bought.

The mother superior said that the bed should consist of a strong canvas cover containing a small mattress, a pillow, two sheets, two blankets, and a mosquito net—especially a mosquito net.

She explained that in Burma, outside of Rangoon and Mandalay and a couple of larger towns, there are no hotels. There are *dak* bungalows, rest houses built by the government along main roads, and *zey-yats,* rest houses built beside pagodas for the seekers after merit, but these are not hotels.

So wherever you go, she stressed, you must take your bed with you. Whether you travel by train, steamer, bus, or bullock cart you are incomplete without your bed. Generally, you will find a place to unroll the bed, perhaps atop a cot or on a table, but usually it will be on the floor. This is the way you sleep, the mother superior said, whether in the house of a fellow priest or a friend, in a tent or under God's sky.

In Mandalay the Columbans were received with enthusiasm. Bishop Faliere, whose society was old, said he was pleased to be associated with such a young society, one founded in Ireland only eighteen years earlier and already attracting vocations from America and Australia. He said the Columbans seemed to him full of enthusiasm and freshness, a description that fitted the six who stood there, each in his mid-twenties and ready for work.

The bishop guided the Columbans on his usual tour which, of course, included the leper asylum. There they noticed a French priest who kept to the background, and when one of their number extended a hand by way of introduction he withdrew with hands behind his back. Later he told of contracting leprosy in Pondicherry. He said that his disease was in such an advanced stage that he had lost all feeling in the decaying extremities. His only fear was of the marauding, hungry rats, scurrying about as he tried to sleep; they could gnaw on him in the dark and he would not feel it.

The visitors walked among the lepers with unease. They would have felt even more apprehensive had they known that in this asylum one of their number would be killed.

Neither the bishop nor his priests tried to gloss over the difficulties that awaited the Columbans. Malaria, of the deadly cerebral type, was the thing to fear most, they said. Old records show that of the fourteen priests serving in Bhamo between 1872 and 1900, only one escaped serious illness or death, and that one was spared because no sooner had he arrived than he was recalled to Mandalay.

Language was a problem, they said, but that could be overcome in time. Travel was frustrating, made difficult by monsoons, the nature of the terrain, and the fact that villages are small and widely scattered.

The French missionaries spoke of Kachins, Shans, Nagas, Was, Karens, Burmans, and Chinese. Give most of your attention to Kachins and Shans, they advised. Especially to the Kachins, who seemed ready for conversion.

The Columbans boarded a paddle steamer of the Irrawaddy Flotilla Company on its way to Bhamo. The first thing they saw was a sign announcing that a third-class passenger was entitled to a space on deck three by nine feet. As second-class passengers they spread their new bedrolls on the bunks of three tiny cabins.

Traders seemed to live on the deck. After buying merchandise in the larger towns, they sold it at smaller towns when merchants came aboard. At each stop passengers embarked with pots and pans, squealing pigs and squawking chickens, to replace the passengers and pigs and chickens that had just disembarked.

From the deck of the riverboat—with its "chunkin' paddles" immortalized in Kipling's poem—the missionaries first beheld a true tropical dawn. The velvet sky changed ever so slowly to indigo, to purple, to violet, to pink, to gold. Then suddenly it burst into burnished brass to let loose on the unprotected decks the full power of the tropical sun.

Passing paddy fields, bamboo villages, and dense jungles the Columbans tried to guess the tribe of each person who came in view: That fellow on the bullock cart, is he a Kachin? Maybe a Shan? Or a Burman? The Kachins were the ones they were really looking for.

By the time the six priests reached the insubstantial jetty at Bhamo, their eyes ached from the glare of the sun and from the strain of look-ing. How delighted they were to see two white soutanes on the dark brown bank. Pat Usher and Bernie Way!

Three creaking bullock carts carried suitcases and bedrolls over two miles of dusty road to Bhamo Town. Darkness came down fast as the journey neared its end. More than forty years later one of the priests would recall: "We were greeted at our unimposing mission house by a solitary French priest, Father François Collard. He bore a smoking oil lamp. It shed little light on a very dark scene."

Three

UPHILL WORK

The darkness of the scene was not something the young priests commented on, but Father Usher knew how they felt. Shortly before their arrival he had admitted to Father Way: "The first night in Bhamo my heart went down to my boots. When I saw this old dilapidated house I said to myself, "What is the rest like!"

The place was shabby and dirty. Downstairs most of the area was work space, except where a wall enclosed a small dining area. The verandah was the community room. Upstairs there were only three bedrooms. And then there were the bugs and the fleas.

What lifted Patrick Usher's spirits was his first visit with Father Charles Gilhodes in a village called Hkudung, 3,000 feet above Bhamo. The Columban later wrote, "He was alone in a part of the country which must rank high among the lonely places of the world."

When the old French priest heard that two new missionaries wished to visit him, he sent down a guide with ponies. This form of transportation was new to Father Usher, at the time. He wrote a description of his pony:

"Mine reached almost to my hip and it seemed brutal to mount him. I was amazed at the sure-footed ease with which the little animal carried me upward for two and a half hours. I was grateful, too, for his smooth, steady pace. Small though he was he had a dignity of his own and did not grudge me mine."

The two Columbans took delight in the six-mile ride up and up. The tiny path, hardly a yard wide, picked its way along the steep incline, curving and twisting and wiggling and squirming. On the right the jungle towered, and on the left a stream hurried through the valley. From all sides came incessant buzzing and occasional bird calls: the voice of the jungle.

In that remote village, the visitors were surprised to find a thousand

Catholics. They also found the Franciscan Missionaries of Mary operating an orphanage and school for about three hundred children, and a dispensary that treated fifty cases a day. These were the sisters Father Gilhodes spoke of years later when receiving the Order of the British Empire. Asked on that occasion what was the greatest gift he had brought to the Kachins, the old missionary answered, "The sisters. Bringing them to the Kachins was the finest thing."

The children of Hkudung were out to meet the two Columbans as they came riding into the village. In their own brand of English they extended greetings, and the smallest of the lot stepped forward to hand Father Usher a letter which he treasured:

> Dear Rev. Fathers,
> We the people of Kachin Hills, old, yeng, thin and fat are all gath-
> ered hear today to pay our best wishes to you, which gushes out
> from the bottom of our hearts. We are very glad to see our good
> shepherds who have come to tend the flock of the Kachin Hills
> from a far nouble country named Ireland.

The date, November 4, was the feast day of the pastor, who had made sure that the celebration was not focused on himself. He had his parishioners so arrange the festivities that it would seem everyone had gathered just for the visit of the Columbans.

The welcoming ceremony took place in front of the boarding school, a warren of wooden buildings with zinc roofs, and all higgledy-piggledy. Here a classroom was stuck on and there a dormitory was attached to a dining room but at a different level. Stairways and verandahs ran up and down and back and forth at various plateaus. Among all of this visual to-do, more than two hundred boarders were getting an education.

In this remote spot, 3,401 feet above sea level, Father Charles Gilhodes had arrived in 1903 suffering indifferent health and totally ignorant of the Kachin language. In a small hut in the village he lived for thirteen years without a convert.

"What did you do all of that time?" asked Father Usher.

"I said the rosary."

In addition to praying he made a close study of the Kachin language and customs, the basis for his book which, in France, was widely acclaimed for its scholarship. Gradually the barriers came down. The opening wedge was a special French dictionary, one that showed a little sketch of everything that could be illustrated.

He would start with the children, he thought, for they seemed to have nothing to do. He would teach them while they taught him.

The start was disappointing. The children had never seen a white man, nor one so bearded, nor one wearing such a strange white robe. When he approached they ran.

Father Usher asked the frail old man, "How did you gain their confidence?" He was thinking of the hundreds of bright-faced children who had just greeted him.

"Bon bons," said Father Gilhodes. "I went to the nearest large village and bought a box of them. The next time the children fled I threw a handful of bon bons and withdrew and waited. Before many days they were coming to meet me."

The language lesson began with the simple objects seen all about: houses, trees, hills, chickens, dogs. Each sound was patiently noted down and memorized. When the supply of local objects failed, the illustrated dictionary came into use. You cannot draw the verb "to be," nor simple necessary notions like "how" and "why," but such expressions are sure to occur often enough to be singled out and recognized. Little by little the French priest and the Kachin children traded vocabularies.

Father Gilhodes, appalled by the disease rampant among Kachins, decided that an unbalanced diet was a major problem. He wrote for seeds to Europe, India, and several countries of Southeast Asia. By experimenting he found which took most kindly to Kachin soil. Eventually, when orchards and gardens grew throughout the district there was a noticeable drop in disease and in infant mortality.

How might the Kachins earn enough income to allow for a dignified standard of living? Father Gilhodes grappled with that one for a long time. When he decided to sponsor the first coffee and tea plantation on Kachin land, he opened a new chapter in Kachin history.

That visit to Father Gilhodes was just what Patrick Usher needed. The feeling of defeat that had oppressed him that first night in Bhamo was somewhat dispelled. What was left of the dark mood faded further during a visit to another French missionary, the dynamic Father Claude Roche.

A few days after this second visit, Father Usher wrote: "In a village about ten miles from this town of Bhamo is a church which, considering all the circumstances, must be seen to be believed. One approaches it by a clay road which is good, as they go, for most of the year. Then for three months the heavy rains come down, the surface is turned into a muddy wallow and the bullock carts plow their way through. When the rains cease the road quickly hardens again but retains a record of each wheel that has passed. The holes are often more than a yard deep, and speeding in any kind of vehicle is not advisable.

"The houses on the way are timber-built, some of them quite neat, others less so. All have the appearance of perpetually struggling with the surrounding woods for their place in the light and air. Suddenly the road enters a wide square in what seems the heart of the forest and there, confronting one, is a fine brick-built church. So unexpectedly it comes into view that it seems a dream. And so it is, a dream come true."

Six hundred and fifty thousand bricks went to form the shell of it. When the pastor began planning the church he lacked bricks, brickmakers, and masons. A book on brickmaking and bricklaying helped him start realizing his dream.

An abundance of clay suitable for brickmaking was near the site. The first attempt was unsuccessful, but, learning from mistakes, the pastor and his parishioners were soon making almost perfect bricks. Men were picked and trained as masons. No tools. With one sentence the pastor set the policy in this matter: 'All tools have been made by men, and what has been done can be done again."

No architect. No construction manager. No contractor. The pastor gave himself all three jobs.

Up went the church. Difficulties were overridden one by one as they occurred. A belfry, one hundred and four feet high, arose with a grace that many an architect might envy.

Every timber in the church was shaped on the spot. All furniture was fashioned by pastor-trained workmen.

A fine statue high above the main door caught Father Usher's attention. The pastor said that a friend of his had sent it from Paris. Poor St. Michael had suffered a mishap somewhere between the warehouse of the Paris packer and the jetty at Bhamo. He arrived with his face a ruin and only the nose intact. Never mind. The pastor, assuming another role, repaired the face so well that from the ground the disaster is undetectable.

Within the church eight strong columns support the roof—discarded rails from a train line. Bases and columns are adorned with mouldings, leaves, and flowers. In the old days teak would have been used but that durable wood is no longer plentiful and cheap, the pastor said.

Short pieces of the railroad track were needed to support the altar rail. The craftsman chosen for the operation refused to believe that it is possible to bite through metal with a tiny saw. He was persuaded to try and, to his amazement, he was successful. In his delight he had all the neighbors and all the wayfarers assemble to behold the marvel.

For the front of the altar the pastor had his heart set on a lamb, one with a pennant over its shoulder, a common feature in church decorations in those days. Since he had to go off to a distant village, he left a careful sketch for the artist to follow. In that neighborhood there are no lambs, but plenty of goats, and so the artist decided that the pastor was trying to draw a picture of a goat. Now he himself liked to see massive horns on a goat, and so taking pains he made them generous enough to be noticed and commented on. Until the pastor returned. With the deft use of a saw the operation was successful.

In telling the newly arrived Columbans about the glories of the church, Father Usher said: "The entire village is Catholic. Besides the church there is an orphanage for fifty boys and thirty girls. A school for catechists. A home for the aged and the infirm. A rest house for travelers. And a well. After the church, the well is the apple of the builder's eye. Not the well so much as the hexagonal roof which shades it. The pastor claims that such a roof is an architectural triumph."

At the first spiritual retreat ever given in the Kachin Hills, Father Usher spoke at length to the young priests about the difficulties the French missionaries had endured. He quoted from Ecclesiasticus: "My son, if you aspire to serve the Lord, prepare for an ordeal."

He brought the retreat to a close with words that he lived by during all of his years in Burma: "I know that God gives his grace in proportion to the work he asks us to do. If I didn't believe that I would shrink from the task.

"We are a small rather helpless bunch of inexperienced missionaries. We know little of the language and less of the customs of our people. In a human way we have nothing to recommend us or guarantee any measure of success. But we do, or at least ought to, possess a mighty weapon of the spirit—Charity. Love. If we have that, God's work here will prosper. If we haven't that, let's pack up our bags and go home!"

Four

IN THE HILLS

The higher Patrick Usher climbed into the hills the higher his morale climbed, too. He was developing an affection for Burma and its people. This shows in the enthusiastic letter sent to the young men who would be coming out in 1937.

"Travel is absolutely gorgeous in the part of the country I have seen. We have three towns in a territory the size of Ireland. They are linked together by either rail or river, and for some miles around each of them there is a bus service. After that you take to your feet or your pony and immediately all the troubles of civilization drop from you. No more post or telegraph or other messages to recall you. You may wear what you like, and think, say, sing, or do what you like.

"It matters little to you that the clothes of today will not be fit to be worn tomorrow, so thoroughly will you have perspired. Across your pack-pony's back two creels are slung, one of which carries your portable altar, the other two blankets and a pillow.

"You will be wise to carry some tins of milk, coffee, sugar, cooking utensils, a supply of 'smokes' and some medicine for distribution. Your space for changes of clothes is very limited, and you give up with regret your idea of bringing a camp bed and a small mattress. The floor will have to do; in this country there is not much danger of catching cold from it. Only your hip and shoulder will suffer for the first few nights.

"You take another glance at your list of essentials and by dint of looking at it you discover that nothing is really necessary except the food and smokes. You pack these with your altar and your blankets, you cram a few pairs of socks, a towel, and shaving gear into the bag slung over your shoulder, and off you go in classic picnic fashion. You have the picnic feeling all of the time you are out."

Father Usher's inquisitive mind and quick eye found delight in exploring the hill country. The first day out he observed that terrain and weather have much to do with the size of Kachin villages. There might be a half dozen houses on a hill considered unhealthy, or on a severe slope, or where rainfall is overabundant. In more benign locations the village numbers more than a hundred houses. The average size of a village is about twenty houses with five persons to a house.

When Patrick Usher first heard French missionaries speak of villages, he pictured a street with houses in neat rows on either side. Right off he found this not true and he wrote: "Level spots to build on are none too plentiful and the Kachin does not like to be crammed up against his neighbor. So you have a ledge with three or four houses on it, a blank while you work your way down a dizzy slope, next a shelf with a single house, then around a knob of a hill to a few more, and so on."

As the Columban rode along on his pony he kept an eye out for a likely place to establish a mission church. Some promising spots were vacant because a house there had been destroyed by fire. When that happens the Kachin believe an evil spirit abides on the spot and no one will build on it while the memory remains. Sites considered unlucky are given to Catholic priests for mission stations, Father Gilhodes had said.

The old man had also told Father Usher that no matter how small the village a Kachin never lives far apart from the rest, for to do so would be tempting thieves. If a thief makes his way into a village, an alarm is sounded and he finds it difficult to make an escape. Men, women, and children are instantly brandishing weapons. The torches in their hands lurching in the night reveal a fearsome array of guns, swords, spears, and cudgels. If the thief is caught he will live to be handed over to the police, but will feel distinctly sore for a long time, so sore that the magistrate's sentence will be mild by comparison.

Father Usher never described the squalor of a village, but how he felt about the first sight of it might be guessed from something Father Timothy Connolly, superior general of the Columbans, wrote: "Somewhere in a Burma rectory I saw a book written by a French priest. It was called *Mission to the Poorest*. I did not feel an urge to read it. The writer, I presume, meant by the poorest the so-called proletariat of the cities of France. If so, he starts with a false presumption; he does not know the jungle slums. Compared with them the slums of a European city—and I have had some experience of the slums of East London in the old laissez-faire days—enjoy a high standard of living."

In those days, before the war, village houses tended to look alike—a wooden frame filled in with bamboo walls and a roof thatched with elephant grass. Each was mounted on posts about six feet tall leaving an open space beneath to shelter pigs. Buffaloes, cows, and ponies had a separate extension attached to the back. Stairs from ground to verandah were not elaborate: sometimes a bamboo ladder, but often six-inch boards notched in a way that the toes of bare feet might grasp them.

At the first house that Father Usher visited a corner of the verandah was closed off as a chicken coop. He entered through the main door, aware that if he entered at the rear he would give offense to host and to household spirits, at least that is what the French priests had told him. Inside he avoided the sanctuary of the spirits, a place off limits to strangers.

The atmosphere was heavy with gloom and smoke for lack of windows and chimneys. Light came in through two doors and the smoke of four hearths filtered through the grass roof.

Since village houses lacked furniture, Patrick Usher sat on the floor, an uneasy position for a tall man with long legs. On the floor in front of each diner was placed a packet of rice wrapped in banana leaves. The curry for adding flavor was served in a common dish, with all present dipping in.

Kachin food in those days would little satisfy gourmand or gourmet, for it was neither plentiful nor varied. All meals were practically the same—rice and curry. The latter was not the exotic, spicy dish blamed for giving British colonels red faces and bad tempers, but a watery concoction of boiled vegetables. On special occasions, ox, buffalo, pork, or chicken might be added.

While the priest dined, his pony ate a feed of paddy, as unhusked rice is called. Paddy is not a Kachin word, but an English rendering of a Malayan word meaning rice.

Upon reaching a village, Patrick Usher found it easy to locate the house of the chief because it was longer than the rest. Since a chief gives himself no airs, nothing about him distinguishes him from other villagers on an ordinary working day.

Respect for his rank, however, is great. The people till his fields and pay him a small tribute in kind to meet expenses incurred on their behalf. Tradition fixes what is due to him on every occasion. For advice he depends on a council of elders whose qualifications are mature years and common sense.

The chief and his elders settle all minor lawsuits. The fees for their troubles are several rounds of drinks provided by the litigants. The judges confine themselves to finding the facts. When these are brought to light, all they need do is apply traditional law, which is not written but handed down by word of mouth from generation to generation. Fines are assessed in cattle, spears, cooking pots, and other things in daily use.

The chieftain and his council decide in January which piece of land should be cultivated that year. The shrubs, vines, and trees on it are cut and allowed to dry for several months in the sun before being set on fire. From the fire, lighted by a man named, Ma Tu, and a woman, Ma Htu, the names of the *nats* who first produced fire, come the ashes that form a fertilizer for the new rice crop.

After harvest, that particular plot of ground lies fallow for ten years. If anyone is tempted to tamper with this cycle, a chieftain said, he need only look across the border into China to see the dire results when land is pushed too hard. There, under pressure of population growth, trees on the hills were uprooted and the land cultivated year after year, until crops grew lean and rain tore away the soil.

"Now those hills are barren of crops and of people," the chieftain told the priest.

Father Usher was pleased to observe how, when Kachins are confronted with nature, they know the wisdom of appeasement. They plant millet at the edge of fields because birds prefer it and so leave the rice alone. Sesame is planted throughout the field so that insects will gorge themselves on it and spare the crop.

The Kachins also know how to let nature work for them in preserving food. After a good day's hunting they pack meat into green bamboo cylinders which they bury in a river bed. Under water, even in a tropical climate, the meat will stay edible for at least six months.

Up in the hills Father Usher found each village something of a closed circle. Strangers are excluded because land is common property and so is not for sale. Despite exclusiveness the tribesmen are most hospitable.

Father Usher wrote: "No description of the Kachins, however sketchy, would be complete without a reference to their splendid spirit of hospitality. Among his own people a Kachin never becomes an outcast, never goes hungry or lacks shelter. Every harvest time the villagers bring presents of rice and vegetables to their chieftain, who reserves them for the entertainment of guests, wayfarers, and travelers who may chance to pass through. A Kachin can travel from one end of his country to the other and be assured of free food and a lodging all the way."

Limits were set on such hospitality. Sister Fidelma, a Columban, wrote a decade later: "If you remain for a day only, you get bed and food gratis, but if your stay is a longer one, you must join in the work. Either you work with the men making baskets, fishing nets, and mats, or felling trees, or with the women pounding rice and gathering leaves on which rice is served."

Besides the word "hospitable," Father Usher often used the words, "loyal" and "friendly" when describing the hill people. Between the priest and the Kachins it was a case of love at first sight. This produced a high morale so infectious that in time Father Connolly, the superior general of the Columbans, would be able to write: "I have just completed a four-weeks' tour of our mission stations in North Burma. Nowhere in the world have I come upon priests and people in closer and more friendly contact."

Five

LEARNING THE WAYS

What a humbling experience, after twenty years of schooling, to be classified as illiterate! The Columbans laughed and cringed when they heard about the Burman census taker who wrote in his report: "Two Catholic priests, both illiterate." So the eight "illiterate" Columbans began steeping themselves in exotic Burma, its language, and ways.

The country was still part of the British Empire, but English was seldom spoken except by foreigners and officials. Of the 130 languages, Burmese was the one used by government-aided schools and by the more sophisticated people of lower Burma. In remote upper Burma, where the Columbans worked, the principal languages were Shan and Kachin.

Although the missionaries would have little use for Burmese, Patrick Usher felt he needed some facility with the official language, and so he and Father McAlindon went to a village near Mandalay to study. Fathers Cooney, Kehoe, and Murphy went to Nanghlaing, nine miles from Bhamo, for Shan. Fathers Way, Stuart, and Walsh climbed the hills to learn Kachin from Father Gilhodes in Hkudung.

No Columban studied the language of the most feared hill tribe, the Nagas. They are head-hunters who believe that evil spirits destroy a rice crop unless fresh heads are impaled on bamboo poles and set in the village as a token of respect for the spirits.

Languages of the Far East are awkward for Western tongues, as the new missionaries soon realized. They found Shan more difficult than Kachin because of its subtle tonal demands. Since Shan is limited to words of one syllable, and there are not enough syllables to take care of all needed words, the difficulty is overcome by varying the tone. A word may be spoken in five different tones, each giving it a different meaning. *Seu* is tiger, if said with an even sound. Said gruffly it means straight. Sung at a high level and stretched out it says happy. Sung high in a staccato it means buy.

In Kachin there are also tonal problems, but not so great. *Wa* may mean man, father, bamboo hut, tooth, or pig, depending on the intonation. *Sa* may mean go, come, rest, or several other things.

Embarrassment resulted from a clumsy use of language. For example, the Kachins have three words for rice in its different stages. Unhusked it is *mam,* husked, *n-gu,* and cooked, *shat.* A missionary might ask if the *mam* is cooking, using the first term when he should have used the third.

On one occasion, when an important animist, a religious leader called a *dumsa* in Kachin, joined the Church, the Columban repeatedly referred to him in a short talk as a big *dumsu.* Each time his catechist flinched because *dumsu* means cow.

A misplaced idiom could also cause a misunderstanding. A Columban noticing that the milk had spoiled told the table boy to throw it out. The boy went to the second-story window, shrugged, and threw out the jug which smashed on the rocky ground. The missionary's Kachin was correct, but he had said "throw out" when he should have said, "pour out."

The young missionaries soon learned that the rosary in Kachin takes much longer that the rosary in English. That is because the language is full of lengthy honorific titles and these are generally used in any formula of prayer.

"This has its drawbacks," a Columban wrote, "when it comes to encouraging the Catholics to say the family rosary every night. It is hard to expect them to spend twenty minutes on their knees. And I mention it in passing merely as an example of the innumerable minor problems which face the missionary every day."

During those months of study the French missionaries told the young priests that they would find the Kachins more easily converted than the Shans. Their prediction was so true that twenty years later, Father Timothy Connolly, the superior general of the Columbans, wrote home from Burma:

"The Shans are Buddhist and extremely difficult to convert. Buddhism has a hold upon them not at all dissimilar to the hold the Emperor of Japan had upon the prewar Japanese. It is so bound up with their social life that to break away from it involves the compulsion of making new friends and trying to enter a new social atmosphere as different from the old as for a European to become an Arab."

The Columbans studying in Nanhlaing learned that Shans are divided into Shan-Burmans and Shan-Chinese. The former go back far into the past and are aware of the days when they had an empire of their own. The Shan-Chinese came to Burma early in this century, crossing the border from China in search of living space.

Although both groups are Buddhists, the Shan-Burmans are the more difficult to convert. For that matter, in any Buddhist village it is not easy for a pagan to become a Christian—so many things stand in the way. For example, difficulties arise when the Buddhists collect money for a local monastery. If the Catholic refuses to give, he is intimidated, sometimes openly and sometimes indirectly, with threats of expulsion from the village. He won't really be expelled, but he will be made to feel unwelcome.

How difficult it is for a Buddhist to become a Christian struck a Columban forcibly while visiting in Mogok. He observed a Buddhist celebration that lasted several days, centering around a recently deceased abbot whose body was enshrined in a gilt casket and placed in a temporary pagoda. The whole countryside gathered around all day and into the small hours of each night to commemorate his "going back."

There was singing, dancing, acrobatics, and dramas. Wealthy people gave day-long feasts to all who would come. It was comparable to a Latin-American fiesta on a grand scale, but distinctly Buddhist. The Columban, caught up in the atmosphere, realized how difficult it would be for a Shan Catholic not to give hospitality during such times and not to accept it from his neighbors.

Father Gilhodes taught the Columbans about the religion of the Kachins. They are not Buddhists, he said, and so in all of the hill country not a pagoda is to be seen. Theirs is not an organized religion but rather a collection of customs.

The Kachins are animists, believing in spirits called *nats*. Every aspect of life has its particular *nat*. One presides over health and one over disease; one is for a good harvest and another for a bad one. The *nats* most feared are *jahtung*, those who bring bad luck in hunting and fishing; *sawn*, those who cause women to die in childbirth, and *lasa*, those who cause accidental deaths. To assuage such evil spirits a buffalo, ox, or fowl might be slaughtered. A succession of misfortunes could in no time deplete a family's livestock.

When a Kachin begins to think of building a house, he consults the household spirits. The place may be built on an old site unless some misfortune has made that place unlucky. The head of the family takes a clod of dirt from the selected site to a soothsayer who beats it with a small bamboo which he holds in the fire until it bursts. If fibers shaped like a snake are produced, that is the sign that the site is favorable. It is also a good sign if two eggs buried on the spot remain good for a few days. If buried fermented rice does not turn sour in several days, that, too, is a good omen. If water in a bamboo tube is buried in the ground and found diminished in the morning, that is good. After sacrificing a fowl or a small pig to the spirit of the place, the Kachin and his neighbors clean and level the site.

A lucky day, usually in the first quarter of the moon, is selected for roofing and moving in. Friends and neighbors come in great numbers, bearing presents of rice, dried fish, meat, and beer. In the morning the owners enter with solemnity, the husband carrying a box of his most valuable possessions, the wife with her cooking pot and tripod, and friends bringing up the rear with the remaining properties.

A new fire is produced by rubbing two dry pieces of bamboo together, with tiny chips of wood for tinder. When a flame springs up, the soothsayer lights two torches from it. The one burning with lesser intensity is supposed to be malicious and so is thrown far away and told to depart to the ends of the earth. The brightly burning torch, the friendly fire, is carried into the house, with the soothsayer exhorting it to remain friendly forever and to perform well its duties of heating and cooking.

The young men are busy putting thatch on the roof and the girls go about serving beer and water. The old people sit around chatting and making bamboo strips to bind the thatch. When the roof is in place the soothsayer gives the good news to the household spirits and makes them an offering of beer, praying that they will watch over the house and its inmates.

When the time comes to plant rice the question is asked: Is the plot free of misfortune? To test this, a root from the soil is given to a baby; if the child chews it that is a good omen. Next the villagers sleep with the root beneath their bamboo pillows. If they have pleasant dreams they are satisfied, but if they dream of wild animals the ground is unlucky and they search elsewhere.

Father Gilhodes said that all of this concern with the world of spirits should make Kachins ready to accept the message of Christianity. Father Usher agreed and wrote home, "The doctrine of the loving providence of God should appeal to tribesmen burdened with a fear of malignant *nats*."

And so it happened, but it took time.

Six

FIRST CHRISTMAS

Christmas in Burma, especially the first, was a time of mixed emotions for young missionaries. To describe this, it might be well to let Father Daniel Cooney tell of his experience.

On the morning of December 24, Father Usher suggested to Father Cooney that since he was studying Shan he might try making himself useful in a Shan parish between now and the Feast of the Holy Innocents, December 28. So Father Cooney mounted a bicycle and set out for the Shan village of Nanhlaing, ten miles from Bhamo.

The first half-mile went well, for the road was more or less blacktop. For the next nine miles the road was scarcely a promise. Dust stood from six inches to a foot deep, a texture that practically absorbed the bike wheels, forcing the cyclist to a well-beaten footpath at the edge of the road.

"Very simple when you say it," said Father Cooney, "but not nearly so simple to do. The path was narrow. Sometimes it rose well above the surface of the road and when it did I usually unbalanced and tumbled off. Sometimes it stopped abruptly and I had to dismount and switch to the other side of the road where a new path took over."

The road to Nanhlaing seemed much more than ten miles. Just as Father Cooney was wondering if he had lost the way, he came upon a village that featured at its entrance a concrete cross with the words: *Crux mea et spes mea,* painted on its pedestal.

Father Alexis, a Burmese, hurried from the confessional to greet his visitor. One of the first things the pastor commented on was the quality of the road: "Hasn't it been much improved of late?"

"I had no answer for that one," said Father Cooney. "I thought the road could not have been worse. Though I didn't know it at the time I was being taught that the relative values by which I had judged things, especially material things, would have to be revised. It's something all missionaries come to learn sooner or later. I traveled that same road seven or eight months later, during the monsoon season. The dust was all gone, but in its place was mud, gluey mud, of varying depths."

Father Alexis excused himself, saying he must return to the confessional. When the penitents, one by one, came to the rectory to see the stranger, Father Cooney grew painfully aware of how a month's study of Shan is inadequate preparation for a conversation. He quickly used up his collection of conventional greetings: *U lee hu?* (Are you well?) and *Hkao Paw gin yan hu?* (Have you eaten rice?)

The Shans asked a torrent of questions. Father Cooney could tell by the tone of voice and the frequent sound of the interrogative particle, *"Hu."* He felt his face freezing and sensed the Shans becoming bored with such an inarticulate fellow. Soon they departed leaving him with the ache of a faded smile around the edge of his lips.

To lighten the hours which were beginning to weigh on him, Father Cooney leafed through some books stacked on a crude shelf. They were mainly commentaries on theology and some sermons, all in French, except for Black's *Medical Dictionary*. The young priest had never expected to spend so many hours on Christmas Eve reading about ailments, but he did.

When Father Alexis returned from the confessional he asked his guest if he would sing the Mass at midnight. Father Cooney was pleased and scared, all at once, for this was his first *Missa Cantata* ever.

At midnight the Church of St. Michael the Archangel was aglow inside and out. Bright ribbons, gaudy paper, and colored stars created a festive mood. The service opened with the placing of the infant in the crib.

Through the years, Father Cooney remembers how the congregation sang that night. "The volume was tremendous. If the loudness was any indication of sincerity, the Lord must have been pleased. I continued on to say my two other Masses. The congregation stayed on to sing Christmas hymns. The airs were so familiar, but how strange the words to my ears."

Father Alexis said his Masses the next morning. The church was crowded because many of the people who had been there at midnight now returned.

After the morning meal, the Shans came for a visit. They brought gifts of rice, eggs, and bananas. Father Alexis gave them candy.

Father Cooney, being a stranger, attracted most of the attention. Again he was limited to nodding and smiling and feeling his face go stiff all over again. When finally alone with Father Alexis the two priests tried holding a conversation but soon ran out of things to say.

"How unlike the Christmases I had known up to this. The weather wasn't like the weather I had come to associate with Christmas. The Christmas fare was not in the least like the traditional fare at home. Were it not for the Masses, breviary, and crib it could have been any day. The day was long, and thoughts often wandered back to home and friends."

The monsignor had said to stay in Nanhlaing until after December 28, so Father Cooney settled down to days slow and lonely and oppressive. Black's *Medical Dictionary* did little for the spirit.

"I had all sorts of thoughts running around inside my head. The most persistent was whether or not I could ever stick the life of a missionary. It took a conscious effort to stay in Nanhlaing with Bhamo and friends so near."

Not many of his friends were in Bhamo, however, because Father Usher had decided to send them out to Kachin parishes. They, too, were finding that clumsiness with the langugage and a lack of feeling for local customs brings a forlorn feeling.

Since the Kachins were a more warlike people than the Shans, they did everything with more vigor; they even celebrated Christmas with more energy. Starting in the morning of December 24, both Catholics and non-Catholics began arriving from villages scattered through the mountains. Beneath a highly decorated bamboo arch, they made an entrance beating drums, pounding gongs, and clashing cymbals. Any available silence was filled with song.

Everyone was dressed in high style for the occasion. Men wore slate-colored Chinese vests and dark blue trousers that reached just below the knees. Women were highly ornamented: silver buttons adorned their blouses; designs of many colors embellished the heavy fabric of their skirts; and necklaces of pearls, bells, and shells set off the ensemble.

Some boys, having made a six-foot cross, covered it with crepe paper and hung a lighted lantern on it. Then they raised the whole thing on a bamboo pole until it stood forty feet tall and could be seen for miles around.

The church overflowed at midnight Mass. At the consecration, in accordance with custom, firecrackers, guns, drums, and gongs shattered the silence outside the chapel. It was the Kachin way of welcoming Christ into the world.

After Mass the visitors settled into flimsy hostels hurriedly built a few days earlier. These afforded scant protection from wind and cold, and none from rain. The bedding was of straw, the same as used to line the Christmas creche.

In mid-morning came the *zuphpawng,* in which priests, catechists, and elders addressed the people for hours. As one missionary said, "Kachins like to hear themselves talking. When they get going they are hard to stop. Topics range from religion to school attendance, from the need for personal cleanliness to the advantages of having planted both tea and coffee crops."

These harangues usually lasted until dark. The hours dragged for the young missionaries who understood little of the preachment. Like Father Cooney they nodded and smiled, nodded and smiled.

Perhaps Daniel Cooney expressed the feelings of most when he said: "That Christmas was a long and lonely one. I read well into Black's *Medical Dictionary* but failed to find my symptoms. It prescribed no cure for homesickness."

Seven

REBUILDING WITH IMPATIENCE

Rebuilding, repairing, renovating, re-establishing, restoring, renewing. That was the theme of Patrick Usher's early years in Burma. In June of 1937 he wrote to Father Richard Cushing (later Cardinal) explaining why, for the present, it is better not to apply for help to build a new church.

"In the organized places we can carry on with existing buildings. In the rest it would be foolish to put up a permanent structure until a priest has been several years in the district and has had time to consider carefully which village is really the most central. The villages are far apart in difficult, mountainous country, and one could be seriously in error through choosing the site for the central residence, church, and school too quickly.

"There is one old-established place in which there is need of a permanent church, but the pastor, who is old and who will remain with us, advises me to wait until our priests have more experience of the country and are fit to undertake buildings. Besides, if we start with simple things, the people will not get the rotten idea that we are wealthy."

In those early days a missionary might spend months evangelizing a village, everything going well, everybody listening politely, and even agreeing with what is said, but no conversions. The tribesmen feared that sickness, death, or some calamity might befall them if they turned aside from the *nats*. Even families unafraid of *nats* still feared their neighbors, aware that if baptized they might be blamed for every calamity that comes along.

To get established was important, but so frustrating. As Patrick Usher wrote years later: "Everyone knows that it would be quite useless for a stranger to walk into a village and start preaching the Gospel without any preparatory work. As soon as you are well established in a place, however, the contacts begin to come. A boy who has been to your school goes home and talks favorably about you; a workman gets a job near the church and asks questions about it; a village chief sees a Catholic school in another village and would like to have one in his own; a man gets sick on a journey and is cured by the priest's medicine. In ways like these the connections are established."

Sometimes, on rare occasions, converts come out of the blue. Such was the story behind the Church at Namhpalam. About five years before the Columbans arrived, two Kachin families on the plains below Namhpalam decided to become Christians. They had never seen a priest, but they had heard about the Church and they liked what they heard. After visiting a French missionary in Bhamo town, they were, in time, baptized.

Neighbors soon followed in their footsteps. From the plains the movement spread into the hills, and before long catechumens numbered several hundred, a good proportion of the population in that district.

Since the nearest priest lived sixty miles away and could only visit once a month, the Namhpalam villagers asked for a catechist. After the catechist arrived they asked for a teacher, and were told that as soon as the school building was a reality, a teacher would be on the way.

Fifty men completed a two-story building in ten days. The ground floor was classroom and chapel and the upper floor was a priest's residence. It was a typical Kachin structure—bamboo bound with cords and not a nail anywhere. The ground floor was clay and the roof thatched grass.

Such buildings need replacing every ten years. This one was showing signs of disrepair by the time the Columbans arrived. Since the renovation of the Namhpalam building is typical of the work the Columbans faced in taking over from the French missionaries, the project is worth describing in detail.

When Patrick Usher sent Father Thomas Walsh to Namhpalam to see what was needed, he told the young priest that he wished he could send him there to build something permanent in brick or stone, but that would have to wait. The common-sense thing to do right now was to rebuild, repair, renovate, reestablish, renew.

Father Walsh wrote back a report: "Many storms and three rainy seasons had their effect. In a number of places the rough winds pushed aside the more courteous thatch and provided entrance for the rain. The cord which bound the building together had sadly aged. The bamboo floor bore traces of many a downpour. It rose and fell as one walked on it, giving the sensation of being aboard ship in choppy weather. The entire structure swayed to the slightest breeze. It was either restore or build anew. The elders met, discussed for hours and hours, and decided to restore."

The women cut the grass for the new roof and carried it to the school on their shoulders. The young men hacked down a small forest of bamboo, while the old men, under the shade of a tree, slit strips of bamboo to tie on the new thatch.

Everything went well, Father Walsh reported, until the question arose as to what style of thatch should be adopted. One old man waved his arms as he described the building as the pride of Namhpalam, the only one of its kind for miles around. On feast days visitors came from afar; they must be given something to look at, something to remember.

A well-tattooed ancient arose to tell of how his grandfather had long ago roofed a chief's house. Others contributed their reminiscences until nightfall came and still no decision had been reached. The villagers dispersed, promising to arrive early the next morning to finish the work.

"Before the debate could begin again," said Father Walsh, "I led a party onto the roof to pull off the old thatch. We made two unpleasant finds. The first was a chameleon's nest. The Kachins do not like the chameleon; they believe it brings death to young people. I was more interested in the second discovery—a nest of angry bees. We had barely begun to work when they attacked us. The slippery roof had to be negotiated slowly, and the ladder was a rickety affair; so our retreat was not so speedy as we would have wished. Most of us escaped unstung. We dispersed the enemy by waving bundles of burning thatch at them."

Father Walsh, working with twelve men, each responsible for a section, began rethatching the roof just as the old men resumed their debate of the night before. When the elders saw that the thatchers were going ahead, not waiting for a decision, they came forward yelling directions. Each old man selected one of the workers as his pupil, and, while squatting on the ground, shouted up to him some detailed directions.

"The local teacher selected me," said Father Walsh. "I can understand Kachin under ordinary occasions, but the technical terms of the Kachin Thatchers' Union are beyond me. Seeing that I didn't understand, the teacher began to demonstrate for me by actions from below. It looked simple, and yet, after ten minutes I could see that something was wrong. The patch that I had done bore my own special stamp and stood out from all the rest. I climbed to the ground to get a better view of my work, and one look from there convinced me that I had better remain below."

That night, under the newly completed roof, the workers and the advisory board were entertained. After prayers and refreshments, the village storyteller was called in. After being presented with gifts, he chanted the praises of priest and school. Whenever he paused the people, with a long drawn out "Eh," signified their agreement.

His theme for the night was the history of Kachin literature. Long, long ago, he said, the Kachins had books, for when the Creator presented learning to the peoples of the world the Kachins were near the front of the line. After receiving their books of parchment, the Kachins started for home in the hills. The books were heavy and the mountains were far away. In their excitement the Kachins had forgotten to bring rice with them and so when they became hungry they were forced to roast and eat their books. And that, the storyteller concluded, is why to this day the Kachins have no literature.

This story took a couple of hours to tell, and Father Walsh, the weary thatcher, nodded through most of it. When he later reported the incident, Father Usher was amused and had him repeat it to every priest who came to Bhamo. Even though amused, the Namhpalam experience aroused his impatience. He was tired of using words that began with "re"—rebuilding, repairing, renovating, reestablishing, restoring, renewing. He wanted to use the word "new" for a change.

Eight

FRESH FOOTPRINTS

While traveling in the hills on a sharp windy day, Father Usher was caught in a downpour, and the chill from wet clothing developed into double pneumonia. For three months he lay seriously ill. By the time he had fought his way back to health it was Christmas of 1937.

During convalescence, he wrote home: "I am delighted with the number of young priests who are coming out; there is work for an indefinite number. The rate of absorbing men will be slow. An extensive building programme lies ahead. The buildings will be the simplest, reminding one of a cattle shed in a field.

"Carpenters are almost nonexistent. Dragging up materials on the backs of small pack-ponies is an infinite labor. The choosing of a site is the most difficult and risky thing of all."

The young priests to whom he referred were Fathers Jeremiah Kelleher, James Devine, Thomas McEvoy, Kevin Flatly, Thomas Dowling, and James Cloonan.

These six and those who had arrived a year earlier worked in parishes established by French missionaries, an arrangement that did not wholly suit Patrick Usher. He became especially restless after Bhamo was made a prefecture apostolic in early 1939. At that time, the northern area was separated from the diocese of Mandalay and formally transferred from the Missions Etrangers de Paris to the Society of St. Columban. Father Usher became Monsignor Usher and, as prefect apostolic, no longer had to make plans that needed approval of Bishop Faliere.

Patrick Usher felt ready to start making new footprints in the hills for by now six more priests had joined him: James McGonagle, Lawrence Hickey, James Foley, James Doody, Michael Barry, and Edmund McGovern. Four others, Michael Kelly, Lawrence McMahon,

Francis McManamon, and John Dunlea, would soon be on the way.

The monsignor was sure that the focus of attention should be on the Kachins. They occupied the great series of hills stretching across northeast Burma into China's Yunnan province. The border between the countries wandered in and out among the hills so erratically that at some places it was difficult to decide whether you were in Burma or China. There was no difference, however, between the Kachins on either side of the border. The monsignor hoped that, in time, the Columbans might link up with the missionaries on the China side, the Betharram Fathers from the south of France.

But why open new territory at this time? Why not develop Myitkyina, a town a hundred miles above Bhamo, easily reached by train or by boat. The argument haunted the monsignor until he and Father McAlindon went up to survey the possibilities.

Sixteen years later he wrote: "At that time we owned a half-acre of land in Myitkyina on which there was a two-room house for the priest and a small church for a handful of Catholics. A priest used to come by train once a month to say Mass for them."

To give Myitkyina more attention made sense, and yet there was that nagging need to open new territory. He wrote later: "The thing that stands out clearest in my memory was the feeling of dismay."

Patrick Usher felt drawn to the Triangle, a vast, wild, mountainous tract north of Myitkyina. It has the shape of a triangle because two rivers, the Mali and the N'mai, start 60 miles apart up near the Himalayas and Tibet, and tend toward each other during the 120-mile journey south. When they join they form the Irrawaddy, which continues down the center of Burma past Myitkyina, Bhamo, and Mandalay to reach the sea at Rangoon.

Although England had been controlling parts of Burma since 1826, the British made no attempt to put the Triangle under civil administration until 1927, less than a decade before the Columbans arrived. Perhaps they would never have bothered that remote wilderness, except that slavery was practiced there. When the government tried freeing the slaves through negotiation, local chieftains said the British Raj should stop tampering with traditional rights.

In March of 1927, the government sent a detachment of military police, mostly Indian Ghurkas, under command of Captain Maxwell West, to arrange terms for freeing slaves. Upon entering the Triangle, the police began reconstructing a bridge only to find themselves caught in an ambush. Captain West and a Kachin leader were killed and several villages were destroyed by fire.

Soon the Kachin guerrillas disbanded and the chiefs agreed to release slaves if the government would pay for them. The rate settled on was 10 rupees for children, 120 for maidens and young men, and 60 for older people. (A rupee in those days was worth about 30 cents.)

Freed slaves fled mainly westward from the Triangle. Many families gathered together to form villages of their own, especially in the Hukaung valley, a dreadful place destined for an invasion of strangers known as Merrill's Marauders.

In the Triangle the British set up a system of indirect rule. Local chiefs were allowed to keep their authority, but were subject to a *taung-ok,* a native overchief. To this position the government appointed Karui La Doi, a shrewd diplomat who knew and respected Kachin customs. With a handful of local police, he set up a headquarters at Kajihtu, where with remarkable success he maintained order and distributed justice.

The choice of La Doi turned out to be a fortunate one as far as the prefect apostolic of Bhamo was concerned. La Doi was in favor of having the Columbans start missions in his area, and the British saw it as a practical contribution to their plan for "Kachin regeneration."

Early in 1939, Monsignor Usher's pro-prefect, Father Denis McAlindon, and Father James Stuart rode ponies into the Triangle to search out a suitable site for a new mission. After crossing the Mali, a few miles above the confluence, they traveled north for twelve days and then provisions ran out. The Columbans had hoped to buy food along the way, but that was a year of rice famine. So on the long journey back to Myitkyina they subsisted on sweet potatoes and some fish and game.

On this trip the Columbans worked out a formula for estimating the time needed for a journey: two miles an hour up or down the mountain; three miles an hour on the level. This rule-of-thumb was used by missionaries through the years.

In December, when the monsoon was past, Father Stuart, this time accompanied by Father James Doody, made another attempt to locate a site for their work in the Triangle. The mission was still unaccomplished, however, when they returned to Myitkyina for Christmas.

At the beginning of 1940 the two of them set off once more. This time they were better equipped: four boys, four pack mules, and enough food for several months.

This matter of supplies was something the monsignor gave great attention to. Perhaps his thirteen years as business manager at the seminary had taught him to think along such lines.

"The first thing to do when one is thinking of settling down in a new place," he wrote, "is to consider the prosaic matter of supplies. After a man has been settled down for a year or so he can have a garden and fresh vegetables, a few fruit trees, a fowl-run for eggs and chickens, a pig or two, and so on. If he has a decent site and any little aptitude for management it will be his own fault if he cannot make certain of not going hungry. He will still have troubles enough in the kitchen department, but at least the specter of famine will be laid low.

"In a new place it is quite different. One can get rice, probably, and a few strange vegetables now and then; nothing more. The average foreigner cannot keep his strength on that, nor will his health last a month. Therefore, he has to carry along tinned foods to tide him over the first lean period; and it is amazing how they bulk when slung in baskets across a mule's back—along with all the other requisites—and how horribly insipid they are when they have to be eaten a couple of times a day and every day. Therefore, we must hurry up with the farm produce.

"One's pack must also include such important items as salt and sugar. Lighting has to be considered, for there is no twilight here, and darkness comes around six o'clock. Hence so many tins of oil must go in. Household utensils must not be forgotten, since there are no furnished hotels on those long journeys. Thin mattresses and blankets must be brought for the same reason. A box is needed to hold all the requisites for saying Mass, as well as books, clothing, and personal effects when one is going for the first time. A few gardening and carpentry tools, nails, screws, and other miscellaneous odds and ends seem to bulk nearly as much as the rest. A formidable load indeed!"

From January to April Fathers Stuart and Doody covered most of the south Triangle. Wherever they went they found the chiefs and the villagers friendly enough, but there was still some suspicion of foreigners. They found it difficult making the chiefs understand that they were Irish, not English.

At Kajihtu they knew they had found the place. The gracious La Doi made them feel so welcome. Father Stuart scouted for a site for the school, and finally selected the summit of a hill above the village. La Doi assured him he would do his best to get the consent of the chief and the village elders.

The Columbans hurried back to Mytikyina to tell the good news and to pack more provisions. As they started their return journey to Kajihtu the rains came. In the Triangle the bridges wash out at the start of the monsoon season, so the two priests had to take the long way around through Sumprabum.

After seemingly endless difficulties in getting themselves and their supplies across swollen rivers they finally reached Kajihtu. There they settled down in a government bungalow to sit out the rain and to wait for La Doi to complete negotiations with the village elders for the property atop the hill.

In July Father Doody took ill and had to return to Myitkyina. This left Father Stuart alone for two months. Each day he met with La Doi. Some days the *taung-ok* looked hopeful and some days dejected.

Those were difficult weeks for Father Stuart. Later Monsignor Usher wrote of how lonely such times can be:

"There are no Catholics up there as yet, and for that reason the first years of the young priests will be exceedingly hard. The whole consolation of a priest's life, of course, is bound up with the administration of the sacraments: baptizing the babies when God sends them, uniting young couples in marriage, pronouncing the words of forgiveness, distributing the Bread of Life, seeing each of the flock safely off on the last journey.

"To have none of these privileges, but to serve day after long day by standing and waiting is desperately hard—yet there is no other way. Confidence must first be won, and that is necessarily a slow affair in a conservative community.

"Meanwhile the priests will occupy themselves with getting a school built and under way, with that essential gardening and stock-raising, with helping the neighbors in their troubles, with occasional travel to make themselves more widely known. Even so they will have many slow and lonely days."

Finally the elders decided that the Columbans could have fifteen acres atop the hill. There at 3,500 feet above sea level, in an amphitheater formed by steep mountain ranges, the villagers began clearing the jungle. As the tangle disappeared, the site revealed plenty of level places for playgrounds and buildings, and—glory be!—a spring of fresh water gushed from under the rocks on the western slope.

After letting a contract for a bamboo house to be built under the eye of La Doi, Father Stuart started back to Myitkyina. His spirits were up now. He would be seeing his confreres and he had good news for them. New ground had been broken.

Nine

DEATH IN THE FAMILY

Monsignor Usher told Father Stuart that he was sending Father John Dunlea as a replacement for Father Doody. At the last moment, he decided to accompany them to Kajahtu and wrote home: "It is part of my work to go to see things myself. Then I understand them in terms of location, and of energy expended, and I note the difficulties."

The trip started well, but ended in a way no one had expected. The 131 miles to Sumprabum, ten mule stages, went without incident. The three Columbans, riding along on their ponies, were aware that the jungle tangle concealed tigers and panthers and the "big three" of snakedom: cobras, kraits, and Russell's vipers. Yet the abundant wild life was mostly invisible. As an American soldier would say four years later: "In the jungle what you see most is the noises."

The jungle, with all its thickets and tangle and profound shadows, is a frightening, chaotic place. It lacks the majestic grandeur of the forest. Fortunately, much of the journey was through dense forests of teak trees, standing to tremendous heights to form a dark vault that blacks out the sky.

A Kachin mule handler told the Columbans much about the trees that they did not know. Green teak, he said, will not float. And since floating is the only way to transport it from remote forests to the mills, trees are killed by being ringed to the heartwood and left standing for three years while the timber dries.

The girth of a tree that is ready for market is six or seven feet, which means the tree is about 150 years old. Elephants drag these massive logs to a stream. The Kachin said the elephants are worth about 5,000 rupees each and need at least four months of rest each year.

Once in the stream, logs are lashed into rafts. Lumberjacks ride them down the Irrawaddy to Mandalay, where some are shipped by train and others floated to Rangoon. It may take from three to five years to get a log from forest to mill.

The Columbans found this early part of the journey so idyllic that the monsignor said of it later: "With our laden mules we had to travel slowly. Glorious weather, delightful scenery, mountain air, and good rest houses maintained by the government along the way combined to make the greater part of the journey a perfect holiday."

The perfect holiday ended at Sumprabum. Although Kajihtu was only thirty-eight miles away, only three mule stages, two swollen rivers lay ahead.

"We had very bad luck," wrote the monsignor.

"The rainy season was well past and good weather was almost a certainty. Not this time, however. Two days and nights of a continuous downpour raised the rivers into enormous roaring torrents full of heavy driftwood. No boat would venture across while the floods were at their height, and so it came about that we took eight days to complete that thirty-eight-mile stretch."

During the delay the three Columbans put up at a dilapidated Kachin village. The people were friendly enough, and that was part of the problem: they insisted on serving food to their visitors.

Father Stuart, always one for needling, reminded his companions that the hill people ate snakes, frogs, field mice, and the pupae of various beetles. He had heard that Chins liked boiled dogs stuffed with a sweet, glutinous rice, and Karens consider cats a delicacy.

The monsignor responded by saying that in the Burmese language the words "delightful" and "diarrhea" sound much alike.

The missionaries sat in the doorway of a bamboo *basha* looking out on a dreary landscape. Father Dunlea remarked that he had now been in Burma long enough to have experienced the three seasons: wet, cool, and steaming. The rains come at mid-May and stay until September; the cool season is from November to March, and hard-to-bear humid heat hangs heavy on the land from early April to mid-May.

Inside the basha the smoke and smells and gloom were unsettling. Besides, God's "little creatures" had inherited the place. Don't kill the lizards, Father Stuart told Father Dunlea, they eat the malaria-bearing mosquito. But do kill those things with so many legs; they carry a sting that brings agony for days.

An abundance of fleas brought bubonic plague into the conversation. The missionaries were plague-conscious because of what had happened when the Bhamo bazaar caught fire in 1939. Rats jumped onto food trucks and were soon delivered with their plague fleas all over the area. When the rats began dropping dead by the hundreds, villagers began dying, too. Rat hunts were formed in village after village. While some men pried up floor boards, others clubbed rats as they jumped out. A normal catch was from 150 to 200 rats a house.

While the three Columbans were waiting out the weather, the villagers came to talk and talk. One seemed exceptionally gossipy. Father Stuart recalled one such in Hkudung; he had nicknamed her "The Rangoon Gazette," and her daughter, "The Supplement."

Someone told of the night, not long ago, when "a frog ate the moon." Three Indian bullock-cart drivers, eating rice beside the road near Sumprabum, became so distressed at the sight of an eclipse of the moon that they dumped their rice onto the ground and used the pots and pans as cymbals to scare away the frog. When the moon continued to disappear the Indians sat beside the road and cried.

In this village men fired guns and women and children beat on pots and pans to frighten the frog that was eating the moon. In time, as had always happened in the past, the frog disgorged its victim, and life returned to normal.

When the three priests continued their journey to Kajihtu, trouble rode with them. Monsignor Usher later recalled:

"A peculiarity of this forest path was the number of leeches on it after the rains. They swarmed on the path itself, and on every blade of grass and weed along its sides. Small things an inch long and as thick as fine twine, they stand on their hinder ends waving their heads in the air. A foot passes near them, or any part of man or beast touches the leaf they occupy, and instantly they cling to this new thing. If it be shoe leather they touch, they proceed by a curious head-over-heels movement to find something softer. Arriving at a sock they slip through the meshes and fasten on the flesh.

"The rest of a leech's movements you know: he collects the blood by suction without biting or breaking the skin or causing any irritation to reveal his presence, and how he swells and swells till he drops off, leaving running the surplus blood which he has collected. You first become aware of his activity when he drops down inside your sock, meets with an accident there, and your shoe is full of blood. He does no harm whatever, but he makes a mess and causes fright the first time, before one knows the origin of all the bleeding.

"As soon as one is on the alert very few get past the first defenses onto the flesh, and if one remembers to rub salt on one's socks they are driven off completely. Their antics are more amusing than annoying, though in other places where they attack at night they are a definite menace."

The real menace was not the leeches or the driving rain or the floods. The Columbans did not even recognize it when they reached their destination after eight days of delay. Inside them typhoid fever was incubating.

On his way back to Myitkyina Monsignor Usher developed a high fever but he thought it was malaria. Up in Kajihtu, Fathers Stuart and Dunlea both took to their beds. The monsignor and Father Stuart recovered quickly, but Father Dunlea grew steadily worse.

La Doi found ten men to carry the young priest on a stretcher over the thirty-eight miles back to Suprabum. Counting backwards for the incubation period, ten to fourteen days, the doctor concluded that the priests had caught typhoid from the water and food in the Kachin village where they had waited out the flood.

In the hospital in Sumprabum Father Dunlea grew weaker and his raging fever would not be quelled. He died on November 16, 1940.

The Kachins made a coffin of teakwood and every man, woman, and child in the village attended the Requiem Mass. Afterward they buried John Dunlea atop a hill looking out toward the mountains of China and Tibet.

From this spot Father Stuart had admired the foothills of the Himalayas. Only recently he had told the monsignor that at sunset those peaks are at their best, with contours standing out against a darkening sky and the last rays casting colors that change every moment.

Monsignor Usher had observed: "It is Connemara at its best, repeated on a gigantic scale."

"It's a long way from Cork," James Stuart thought as Kachins filled in the grave.

Once more Father Stuart made the 165-mile journey back to Myitkyina. This time Monsignor Usher told him that his coworker would be Father McAlindon. The two priests hurried to return to Kajihtu, hoping to be there in time for Christmas.

The nearer they came to Sumprabum the more despondent they felt. It would be painful to see the cross on John Dunlea's grave silhouetted against the sky. They stopped to pray at the grave and then pressed on to Kajihtu. They arrived on Christmas Eve.

Outside the village La Doi hurried to meet them. He couldn't wait to report that their new building was finished—at a cost of fifty rupees, about seventeen dollars.

Behind La Doi stood all of the villagers. The priests and the people were no longer strangers; they had shared a universal experience. Each knew deep in the marrow that "It is appointed to man once to die."

Ten

WAR REACHES BURMA

Pearl Harbor! The words echoed even in the wilderness. War came to Burma just as Monsignor Usher thought that things were going well. New missions were opening and the transfer of parishes from the French fathers was about complete. Two more priests had arrived; Fathers Thomas Rillstone, a recently ordained New Zealander, and John Howe, a doctoral student of theology at the Gregorian University in Rome since his ordination in 1936. This brought the number of Columbans to twenty-five.

No one in Bhamo expected the Japanese to pour into southern Burma and race northward so fast. When refugees came streaming up from the southeast, missionaries opened school buildings to house them, and parishioners quickly built bamboo shelters for people who hoped the war would never reach this far.

"May 3, 1942, is a date we shall not easily forget," said Monsignor Usher. At noon a disheveled British doctor hurriedly returned from the front to report that Japanese soldiers were crossing the last bridge approaching Bhamo. He offered the monsignor and Fathers McMahon, Way, and Dowling transportation to India. They thanked him saying they preferred to stay with their parishioners.

When the doctor saw that they had no intention of leaving, he asked if they would take charge of the Bhamo Civil Hospital. Monsignor Usher agreed, wishing in his heart that the burden had not been thrust upon him. The place housed many severe cases of smallpox and was in a state of chaos. How chaotic can be guessed from the fact that the priests discovered several bodies that should have been buried days ago, for in Burma the dead must be interred within hours.

Monsignor Usher assigned Fathers Dowling and Way to stay at the hospital to work with the sisters of the Franciscan Missionaries of

Mary. He told them to protect the medical stores from looters, keep helpers from quitting, tend the sick, and bury the dead.

The Columbans felt forlorn as they watched civil administrators and military men in cars streaming out the north road. The people of Bhamo hurried along every path to seek refuge in hidden villages. By dark the sick and the dying and the missionaries had the town to themselves.

Stores of food and gasoline went up in curtains of black smoke, torn apart in a moment by explosions and tongues of flame. Shells made a fluttering sound passing over the hospital in a barrage that lasted for half an hour. Silence returned only briefly. The chatter of machine guns announced the Japanese entrance into Bhamo Town by the light of a brilliant moon.

It was a bad night, with long silences broken by sudden bursts of firing. At dawn the occupation proper began with tanks and heavy guns rolling in. No one came near the Columban enclosure while the priests were offering a Mass of thanksgiving that the worst was over and they were all alive.

When a Japanese soldier came at noon to search the house, Father McMahon's pyx caused some uneasy moments. The soldier thought the small gold case, used to carry the Eucharist, was a pocket watch. He demanded the inner works that would make the thing go tick-tick. Through sign language the priests tried to convince him that this was a religious object, not a timepiece.

With gestures the soldier indicated that bad things would befall them if they did not produce the rest of the watch immediately. Finally he flew into a rage, stormed from the house, but returned immediately to ransack room after room. At last, muttering in anger, he departed holding the pyx to his ear as though expecting it to start ticking at any moment.

"Apparently the soldiers had instructions to spare our lives," said Monsignor Usher, "for when rifles were levelled at us with seeming intent, the word Christian or the sign of the cross acted like a charm.

"Dusk approached, yet no officer had come to us, so we went out to look for one to ask for protection for the night. By the time we got back, soldiers were occupying our building."

The commander wanted to see the American and the Australian, meaning Father McMahon and Father Way. In a bamboo basha three officers sat on chairs, swords in hand, and the priests stood, surrounded by soldiers. The commander concentrated on the American.

"How is it that we found you in charge of a hospital harboring Chinese soldiers?"

This was news to Father McMahon; he was unaware that wounded soldiers had been left behind. To say this would sound too lame, and so he explained that he had been asked to look after the hospital to make sure that there was no looting before the Japanese arrived.

"Why didn't you leave?"

"Our place is with our parishioners."

This seemed to satisfy the commander. "Don't be afraid," he said. "We are here to protect you."

Throughout the day the question asked time and again was, "Why didn't you run away to India?" The Irish priests tried to explain their position of neutrality, but the Japanese said, "English, Irish, all same."

The Japanese commander said to Monsignor Usher, "The army is taking over your building."

"Where shall we go?"

A shrug. "Anywhere."

The question of where to go was soon answered when the commander decided to put the Columbans under "Protective Custody" in Bhamo jail. He had a way of saying "Protective Custody" that put the sound of a capital letter at the beginning of each word.

The commander must have thought that if the priests failed to flee when they had a chance, they were either fools or spies and in either case might best be confined. He ordered two military policemen and a young Burman, introduced as the head jailer, to herd them, laden with their baggage, to a flea-infested jail.

As the days passed, other Columbans arrived from mission stations. One of the first, Father Flatley, was marched for twenty-three miles across the hills by a native chief who handed him over to the Japanese, saying he had given food and clothing to English officers passing through on the way to India. The priest admitted this. To the chief's chagrin, a military policeman cut away the ropes that were sunk into Father Flatley's wrists and gave him a cup of tea and a cigarette before taking him to join his friends.

When Father Doody was arrested far from Bhamo, the Japanese accused him of being a spy. They tried to persuade him to admit it, and when he would not they tied him up and beat him. That continued for a couple of days before they threatened to kill him. At the first opportunity he escaped into the jungle. After a day he was recaptured and given a few more beatings on the way to Bhamo jail.

A few days later the Columbans were released and interned in a house near the Baptist church.

When Father McGonagle arrived he said that soldiers had disported themselves in his church vestments. After taking his food and clothing, they gave the chalice, monstrance, and pyx to coolies who transported their loot.

As the Columbans came in one by one, they were delighted to find their colleagues interned, for the rumor in the hills was that all missionaries had been executed. As each arrived with a story of adventure, Monsignor Usher drew him out detail by detail. Since Thomas Rillstone later wrote of his experience it might be well to present it here as typical of the kind the others endured.

Father Rillstone's story began before Pearl Harbor. When the British found the war going badly for them in the Far East, one of the things the frustrated authorities did was interne Italian missionaries. The police rounded up those who had been in the country for less than ten years on the grounds that they may have come as spies.

To help replace the imprisoned missionaries, Monsignor Usher sent Father Rillstone to Namtu in the Northern Shan States. After a couple of months the young Columban was transferred to Lashio, a Tower of Babel, where languages heard on the streets included English, Shan, Hundustani, Tamil, Kachin, Burmese, Karen, Chinese, and Telegu.

Arson had become epidemic in Lashio and punishment was exceedingly severe. When a Chinese soldier apprehended an arsonist, the culprit was stripped, bound, thrown into the back of a truck and driven rapidly up and down rough roads until the fellow died.

There were amusing incidents, too. An old Shan loaded a piano and an unexploded bomb onto his bullock cart and headed for the jungle. Two men perched atop the cart, one thumping the piano keys haphazardly and the other beating time on the bomb.

Father Rillstone found himself in the air-raid belt of Lashio. After three hundred raids he quit counting. In recalling them he said, "When the bombs begin to explode the tension is relaxed. It is while the planes are flying about overhead that terror grips your soul. The strain of expectation is nearly always the same."

With bombs, robbers, murders, disease, and worst of all, overcrowding, Lashio became a place to escape from. Each day American transport planes flew refugees to Calcutta, carrying women and children to safety, taking men aboard only when no more women and children were on the tarmac at the moment of departure.

Father Rillstone stood his ground until the Japanese began closing in. He then joined a retreating British convoy for a rough 200 miles from Lashio to Bhamo.

No sooner had he arrived in Bhamo, at two o'clock in the morning, than Monsignor Usher assigned him to help Father Devine in a remote Kachin village fifty miles away. After getting a little sleep, Father Rillstone set out with a retreating Royal Air Force convoy. He rode through the night with them for forty miles to a point as near as the road would get him to his destination in the hills. Upon saying good-bye and thanks at two o'clock in the morning, he settled down in a Kachin hut, not daring to move alone through the jungle with so many tigers abroad.

At dawn Father Rillstone tramped the remaining ten miles up through the hills to arrive in time to say Mass. Father Devine was surprised to see him and delighted for the companionship of a colleague. The delight was short-lived, though, for within a matter of hours life became confusing and unsure even in that remote village. Mysterious bullets whizzed by and Japanese soldiers ransacked the house.

A certain absence of logic developed that the missionaries found maddening. A Japanese officer wrote a permit for a truck to move them to Bhamo, but he refused to write a permit for the gasoline to operate the truck. A military commander ordered them to his office, but a sentry refused them entrance because they lacked a pass, explaining that the person issuing such a pass was the commander himself.

Fathers Devine and Rillstone set out to walk the fifty miles to Bhamo, each leading a pack pony heavily laden with bedding, clothing, food, and Mass kits. On the way Father Walsh joined them.

When Father Rillstone sprained his ankle he had to ride one of the ponies while the two other priests divided the pony's pack load between them for a slow and painful journey. At the end of which they joined their colleagues interned in Bhamo.

Twenty years later Monsignor Usher wrote: "In jail we fared well. The Franciscan sisters managed to maintain contact with the outer world and acquired various necessities. Old friends whom we had helped in better days brought us milk and so on, while our Catholics braved every danger to bring us presents. There were drawbacks, though. We had to attend to sanitation ourselves or risk typhoid. We did not realize how many bugs there can be to a square inch till we found ourselves bitten all over, and set about rooting out the enemy.

"After settling down to make a home in our new quarters, we set up two altars and often had gaping soldiers around us while we said Mass. On Sundays we even reserved the Blessed Sacrament and had benediction. We kept fit by drilling every morning and putting in an hour grinding wheat for bread. We devised games and smuggled in books. Since our destiny was no longer in our own hands, we were completely happy."

On June 18, 1942, the Columbans were released from jail to find the town a scene of desolation. Great tropical weeds had sprung up in the once trim gardens. The wreckage of furniture lay around untended lawns. Dummies for bayonet practice dangled from trees.

The church was in a filthy state, for it had been used as a barracks. Soldiers had pulled the organ to pieces using the woodwork for kindling and the boards of the walls for firewood. While destroying the church, they had also burned the house and school.

"On October 28, the sixth anniversary of our arrival in Bhamo, our hopes ran high," wrote Monsignor Usher. "From Tokyo, in response to representations made by the Vatican, there came an order that we were to be specially protected."

The reaction of the commander in Bhamo was to order all Columbans to start for Mandalay immediately. He probably wanted to be free of the responsibility, or may even have thought that he was being helpful. As it turned out he was doing them no favor.

Eleven

A TWO-YEAR JOURNEY

While most of the Columbans were gathering in Bhamo, a few were still scattered across central and northern Burma. Since Fathers William Kehoe and Michael Kelly were the first to feel pressure from the Japanese army, it might be well to tell their story before moving on to the others.

Monsignor Usher had sent Father Kelly down to Kengtung, a market town, capital of a Shan state of the same name, and the most easterly town in Burma. When war broke out its population was 5,500, compared with Bhamo's 7,800 and Myitkyina's 7,300. Its ethnic mixture was highly seasoned—Shans, Burmese, Siamese, Chinese, Lahus, Ikawas, Was, Karens, and Kachins.

High on a hill sat the mission compound, dominated by a fine main building of red and white trim, and a large church of an architecture found in Italian hill towns. There was also a long, low building that had been used as a seminary until the British army requisitioned it for a supply depot.

At the time Father Kelly left for Kengtung, in June of 1941, Father Kehoe was stationed in a Kachin village, Zaubung, fifty miles southeast of Bhamo. In September, Monsignor Usher told him to join Father Kelly to help in Shan parishes that needed priests now that the British had put most Italian missionaries under arrest.

Kengtung was the terminus of all convoys, and so the truck that Father Kehoe rode stopped there. In the glare of headlights, coolies moved about unloading supplies. Amid much commotion, Father Kelly introduced his colleague to Monsignor Bonetta and Father Portaluppi, elderly men left behind when nineteen younger Italian priests were imprisoned at Kalaw.

Fathers Kehoe and Kelly were embarrassed by the politeness of their parishioners. Shans, both Christian and pagan, never addressed a priest without removing their hats and would not consider sitting in his presence or wearing shoes in his house or in church.

"On Sunday morning," Father Kehoe wrote, "it is almost impossible to step into the church, so great is the pile of shoes outside the entrance. How each one can find his own after Mass is always a puzzle to me, since all look so much alike—just a piece of wood shaped like the sole of a foot with a strap over the instep."

The Columbans were especially embarrassed whenever a parishioner kissed their hands. Even pagans put a priest's hand to their foreheads. Most embarrasing of all was when a Shan kissed the feet to show gratitude for a service rendered. Western culture was not at ease with Oriental courtesy.

The missionaries found that hospitable Shans insist on serving tea and spirits on the slightest occasion. The Shan word for tea means "hot water," an apt description. Spirits, though, are something else: the whiskey is called "tiger's milk."

The new assignment was pleasant enough until Pearl Harbor, when the young priests suddenly became conscious of the Japanese armies on the French Indo-China border, sixty miles away. Since the people of Kengtung believed the armies would arrive in less than two weeks, the mood of the town changed overnight. Easygoing ways vanished as suspicion and fear filled the streets.

Monsignor Usher worried about his two men in Kengtung. As soon as fighting began at the border, he ordered them to hurry back to Bhamo. "It is your duty," he wrote, "and you have no choice."

The letter arrived shortly before the Japanese sent fifty bombers over Kengtung on April 13, 1942. In describing the arrival of war, Father Kehoe wrote: "The desolation in that town, in a raid lasting perhaps five minutes, was inconceivable. Where whole streets had stood before was now nothing but rubble. Everything seemed to achieve the most grotesque attitude possible—houses, lorries, carts, and the dead. In all there were about 500 casualties. All that day we worked in the broiling sun with bands of coolies who had almost to be driven to it, digging out the dead and dying. As we worked, friends and relatives stood around with dazed and shocked looks on their faces.

"A party of soldiers, who seemed to realize for the first time how real and sudden death can be, came calling for the priest. Father Kelly and I, caked as we were with dust and sweat, had to leave aside our picks and shovels and retire to a quiet spot amid the ruins to hear their confessions.

"We took away the dead in lorries and laid them in lines in the hospital grounds for identification, and the wounded we rushed to the few overworked doctors in the hope of saving a life here or there. But it was hopeless. The avalanche of dead and dying loosed on this little town at only a moment's notice was too much.

"The people fled to the jungle and left Kengtung a town of the dead. Bullocks, horses, and dogs had to be shot as they were wandering about with great gaping wounds. Father Kelly and I located any Catholics who had been killed—there were ten in all—made coffins for them and buried them with what ceremony we could."

Word came over the radio that the Japanese were moving faster than even the pessimists had thought possible and that they had cut the road to Bhamo. This left the two Columbans unable to escape the turmoil of southeast Burma. What to do, now that it was impossible to follow the monsignor's instructions?

The outbreak of complete lawlessness was one of the growing horrors. As local governments dissolved and police deserted their posts, the worst elements took over. Vultures began circling in the sky.

Father Kehoe watched with horror as seven Chinese opium smugglers fought to the death outside of the mission house. They were at each other with knives and revolvers until three fell dead on the doorstep. At revolver point Father Kehoe was ordered to remain inside. From there he watched the vultures go about their work. By the following day nothing was left but glistening skeletons and rags that had once clothed bodies.

The Columbans hurried fifty miles north to Mongpawk only to find things getting worse. Japanese and Siamese soldiers and badmen from the border were all coming that way. A Chinese general described the situation and urged the missionaries to join his army in a retreat northeastward into China. With the memory of vultures fresh in mind, they took his advice. At times they would wonder if they had made a wise decision.

The march was a nightmare: three thousand soldiers and two hundred pack ponies. And the monsoon made the mountain trails an agony. Despair was a constant companion during those slow monotonous days surrounded by gray immensities. Father Kehoe recalls, "As we climbed higher into the mountains the rains were beginning, and with the thousands of marching feet and hooves, the road became impossible. We slipped and we slithered. Men and ponies fell. The sick and wounded on their litters groaned and twisted and turned and stared with sightless eyes up into the lashing rain. Many died on the trail. Here and there we passed parties digging shallow graves under the trees. The bodies lay on the ground awaiting their last resting place."

When the priests were across the border into China, they decided to leave the army and take refuge in some part of Burma not yet occupied by the Japanese. They struck northward hoping to find Tapalu where a French missionary lived.

The head-hunting Was were a new danger. Someone assured the Columbans that they only did their hunting at the time of planting. The Was eventually descended in force on a village not forty miles from where Fathers Kehoe and Kelly were visiting the French missionary. After beheading every man, woman, and child that they could catch, they beheaded some of their own tribesmen, nonhead-hunters, known as "tame" Was.

In Tapalu the Chinese magistrate kept the Columbans in house arrest for ten months. Finally, when a new magistrate said they were free to go, they went out to load their ponies only to find that one had disappeared. His mangled body indicated that a leopard had carried him off. Worse still, the lead pony took sick and the rest of them caught it. Three died and, of the two remaining ponies, one was carried away by a tiger.

The missionaries sold their shotgun and radio to get money for food. This, along with a loan from a farmer, and they were ready to start for Kunming, seven hundred miles away.

About then they heard that Bhamo had fallen and wondered if the Columbans were free. Or captured? Or killed? They asked each other that a thousand times, realizing they would not know the answer until the war ended—and Lord knows when that would be.

The trip from Tapalu to Kunming seemed like a time set apart for discouragement. So many things went wrong. Halfway across a suspension bridge a pack pony panicked and started to gallop; the swaying bridge tossed him over the side and he disappeared into the churning waters. A few days later the muleteers sat down and refused to move forward another step. The Columbans had to shoulder their belongings and go on without them, not knowing what had caused the sudden strike. Besides, this was country in which bandits prospered, and where no meat is fried at night because the aroma attracts tigers.

Of the six-week journey, the last three days were by truck over the China section of the Burma Road from Siakwan to Kunming. Even this was a hair-raising experience because the drivers grossly overloaded their vehicles.

The Columbans watched trucks leaving Siakwan for several days, hoping to board one properly loaded. They finally realized that they would be there until war's end if they failed to boost their courage enough to take a chance, and so they boarded a three-ton truck that carried twelve large bales of tea. Six of the bales fitted snugly into the body of the truck, and six more were placed on these to reach well above the driver's cab. On top of this rode thirty or forty passengers with their luggage. Inside the cab were two "first class" passengers and the driver's copilot.

"We only took the risk because we had no choice," Father Kehoe said. "Even on an ordinarily level road such a heavily loaded vehicle would be a menace to the safety of its own passengers and to the world at large—and the Burma Road is no ordinary road."

On hairpin turns the missionaries looked down to see the wrecks of trucks that had gone tumbling to their doom. What had happened to the passengers was a thought they tried not to dwell on.

After a month in Kunming the Columbans were flown across the Himalayas to Assam, where they were held in detention for several days until British intelligence could clear them of any suspicion of spy activity.

Finally, in June of 1943, two years after leaving Bhamo, they arrived in Calcutta. Both priests were assigned to parishes—Father Kehoe in New Delhi and Father Kelly in Calcutta. There they worked until the end of the war.

Twelve

TWO HEROES

Had he not volunteered to go southward into the war zone, Father Jeremiah Kelleher would have shared Bhamo jail with his confreres. He was teaching in Bhamo, at a school for catechists, when the Japanese began a serious conquest of Burma. Although teaching was strenuous, the lanky priest generated enough energy to spend his free evenings in the military barracks at the edge of town instructing Kachin soldiers in catechism. By the time the Kachins were ordered to move to garrisons in lower Burma, they considered Father Kelleher their unofficial chaplain, and so did he.

Would it be better at this time to tend the spiritual needs of soldiers or teach catechists in school? With this dilemma he went to Monsignor Usher, feeling deep inside that he should accompany the troops.

"Permission was readily granted," said Father Kelleher. "I also received a letter of recommendation from Colonel Jacob, the commanding officer of Bhamo. The letter helped when I reached Maymyo in central Burma."

At Maymyo he needed all the help he could get. Military headquarters had moved there when Rangoon was on the edge of capitulation, and it was at Maymyo headquarters that he went through two weeks of frustration trying to get permission to enter the war zone. Only if you have a commission from London, he was told. Since communications were so poor, the chances of getting such a thing seemed remote. Eventually, the commanding officer at Maymyo used good sense and appointed Jeremiah Kelleher an accredited officer in the army of Burma.

Immediately, the chaplain moved toward the front. At Meiktila he found some Kachins serving with a military police unit. This seemed to fit into his assignment, for Monsignor Usher had said in parting,

"God speed. Remember that your work will be among the Kachin troops. You are not being sent for any European units. They should have their own chaplains."

Once again, Chaplain Kelleher felt frustrated. Kachins were few and were scattered in units formed mainly of Buddhist Burmans and Hindu and Muslim Indians. He felt he was wasting time searching for Kachins; besides they were doing garrison duty and were not on the front lines.

When Rangoon fell, March 8, 1942, a battalion of the Enniskilling Fusiliers was flown into Magwe. The chaplain hurried to join the Irish soldiers, who moved directly to Prome. The unit is about sixty percent Catholic, said Colonel Cox, of Belfast, upon welcoming the chaplain most graciously.

The Kachins still haunted Jeremiah Kelleher whenever he recalled Monsignor Usher's admonition. Thirty-five years later he explained why he did what he did. "Their need certainly did not seem as great as that of the Irish troops who lived in constant danger in active fighting. Day after day and night after night the Enniskillings fought the Japanese army.

"It was quite clear that we were fighting a losing battle. For this very reason I was happy to be on the spot, deeply involved with the troops in action. This included not only our Fusiliers but many other units of the British army. These men were grateful for my services and thankful for the opportunity of receiving the sacraments."

The soldiers were badly in need of help, for their morale was sinking fast. Three months of bitter campaigning under agonizing hardships had left them enfeebled. They no longer wanted to fight in Burma. The Indians were impatient to return to their native land, and the British had seen as much as they wanted of this forsaken country.

Jack Belden wrote at the time: "Looters, arsonists, brigands, thieves cutthroats, fifth columnists and 'traitors' now swarmed out of the villages into the vacuum created by the retreating allied armies. They overran the roads, laid ambushes, tore up the railways. They pounced upon the towns, setting them ablaze, stealing, killing, terrorizing, and beginning a general reign of chaos and anarchy."

As the Japanese moved into one side of Prome the British troops fled out the other. Now the defeated army began a leapfrog action: some units would cover the withdrawal and then take their turn while those who had pulled back set up new defensive positions. It was an anxious time, with machine-gun harassment on the ground and bombs falling from the air. Casualties were heavy.

On many occasions Jeremiah Kelleher was near death. Once, while traveling in a truck, men on each side of him were killed by machine-gun bullets.

On another occasion when he was left near dead behind enemy lines, a young officer slipped through and brought him out.

"When the Japanese encircled Yenangyaung and set up road blocks our position was critical. Could we break through or could we not? That was the problem. When the oil wells of Yanangyaung were set on fire I could read my breviary at night by the light of the huge flames belching up into the sky. It was a time that I will never forget!

"By now I was not in very good form. The heat of the day and the heat of the night, generated by the oil wells that surrounded us, proved too much. In the last days of April I suffered severe heat stroke and was incapacitated. All the while the battle raged. I could not do very much for the troops and could administer the sacraments only to those who came to the dressing station."

When orders came to crack the encirclement or perish, the chaplain was among the disabled placed on tanks. After several days of hardship, including starvation, the troops made a breakthrough. At the river the sick and wounded were placed on boats belonging to the Irrawaddy Flotilla Company and taken up to Katha.

There the decision was made, on May 2, that anyone well enough to walk should commence the trek to India. Father Kelleher preferred to stay in Burma and so was put on a train for Myitkyina. At the end of the line he would find a fellow Columban, Father James Cloonan, pastor of Myitkyina, or so he hoped.

What he did not know was that Father Cloonan was also doing heroic work. It is described by an Australian Redemptorist, Father L. Carroll. In a letter to Columban headquarters in the United States, Father Carroll told of his experiences in Myitkyina as the war moved closer:

"A real hero, if ever there was one, is Father Jim Cloonan. I owe him a deep debt of gratitude. When I reached Myitkyina after my journey from Bhamo, exhausted and destitute, I found in his little two-room presbytery two priests and four Indian teaching brothers. Yet he made room for me, gave me his bed and his clothes. What a man!

"Besides his own parish, he was attending the refugee camp, where the majority of the thousands of Anglo-Burmans were Catholic, people reduced to the utmost misery and despair. The civil hospital was full to the roof. Train-load after train-load of wounded troops were reaching the military hospital. Father Cloonan met every train, day or night, as it arrived, giving the last sacraments to men who had not seen a priest since the terrible campaign began.

"He was trying to arrange the evacuation of a community of Poor Clares and their aged chaplain. Thank God, they got away! He had on his hands fifteen or twenty Good Shepherd nuns with their school girls from Rangoon, depending on him to provide them with a shelter and food fifty miles away in the jungle in a place of comparative safety. I can assure you that the care of women and girls in the circumstances was no light responsibility; I had a taste of it myself.

"The last I saw of him was when he had received word to remove the nuns immediately. He had been up all night, and his only transport had hopelessly broken down halfway to the place where he had prepared a bamboo convent for them.

"Such utter selfless devotion, especially in one far from being physically robust, surely deserves the name of heroism which I have given it. To work twenty hours a day, with never a thought for himself and the smile never fading from his lips, was heroism of a pretty high order if I know anything about it."

Father Cloonan was not in Myitkyina when the soldiers left their chaplain in the military hospital and moved on. When he returned he searched out Jeremiah Kelleher in the crowded warren of the disabled, and the Columbans made some serious decisions. Fly by air transport to India, as was offered, or stay in Myitkyina? Father Cloonan felt his place was with the refugees, but urged his colleague to fly to safety now that the military units had vanished in disarray. Father Kelleher gave it some thought and decided that he too should work with refugees.

When the Japanese reached Myitkyina on May 9, they were not long in arresting the two priests, the fifteen nuns, and the young girls from Rangoon. All were held in the Baptist mission compound for three months before being sent south to Rangoon, where they were placed under strict house arrest in Kokine, a suburb.

"We spent the remainder of the war years in reasonable comfort," said Father Kelleher. "We had no great problems nor were we molested in any way. Food and other daily necessities were difficult to obtain, but the friends of the sisters were very good to us, generous and kind."

Columbans at their headquarters in the United States and in Ireland were concerned about the fate of Fathers Kelleher and Cloonan. They hoped that both were with the Columbans being held at Mandalay. The last word concerning Father Kelleher had come through Michael Dennehy, of the Enniskilling Fusiliers. While convalescing in India the soldier Dennehy had gone to St. Joseph's College, at Coonoor, in the Nilgiri Hills, to give information that was passed on to the apostolic delegate.

In a written statement, the young man from Tralee said: "He was generally to be found, when not attending the wounded, in the front line with the men fighting the rearguard action. He was in turn priest, stretcher bearer, nurse, and doctor. He comforted the living and buried the dead, so much so that, dressed in rags and shaking with fever, when he reached Myitkyina the doctor pronounced him unfit to travel any farther. The men of the battalion offered to take turns carrying him until such time as they would find a pony or reach Assam, but he refused to burden them, saying that he would be all right and that his place was with the wounded and in rendering what help he could to the stragglers and the evacuees."

There was a sense of dismay among Columbans when Fathers Kelleher and Cloonan were not among missionaries released from Mandalay in March of 1945. That they were safe was not really known for sure until the British reoccupied Rangoon two months later. On May 29 a cablegram reached the Columban headquarters at Navan in Ireland:

"Fathers Kelleher and Cloonan liberated in Rangoon. Both well."

Thirteen

CREATING LEGENDS

While Mandalay, Myitkyina, and Bhamo fell like dominoes, Fathers Stuart and McAlindon were safe in the Triangle, up in Kajihtu, but not for long. Before anyone expected it, refugees came swarming across the hills just ahead of the Japanese army.

The two missionaries hurried the school's sixty boarding students back to their homes in the scattered villages and after that gave full attention to the refugees. Food, housing, and medicine were always scarce, of course. Whenever the frightened refugees felt fit enough to continue, the Columbans provided Kachin guides to lead them to places that seemed safe, at least for the time.

The horrors that refugees endured in those days cannot be exaggerated. Dr. Gordon Seagrave wrote of their plight in *Burma Surgeon,* the story of his trek with Stilwell to India. In *Burma Surgeon Returns* he tells of what he saw when coming back over the route two years later:

"From the first day on we passed skeletons in ever increasing numbers, yet we could see evidences of camps, where, by setting fire to shacks, hundreds of skeletons had been destroyed en masse. There were skeletons around every water hole, lying sprawled out where the refugees had collapsed. At the foot of every ascent were the bones of those who had died rather than attempt one more climb, and all up the hills were the bones of those who had died trying. Still standing along the road were some extremely crude shacks, each with its ten to twenty skeletons of those who couldn't get up when a new day came. In one shallow stream we were horrified to find that the Chinese had placed a long row of skulls to be used as stepping-stones. Sex and age and even race could be noted, not by such elusive clues as surgeons use but by the rotting clothes. When I saw a skeleton clothed in a delicate English dress I was thankful for Tiny's departure a year before. Looking at the skeletons of little boys in khaki shorts, I realized they might have been John or Sterling. There were men, women, and children of every race and age, their hair white, gray, brown, black, still lying beside the whitened skulls; there were English, Anglo-Burmese, and Indians—civilian and military."

Refugees who came upon the two Columbans were fortunate because after two years in the Triangle, Fathers Stuart and McAlindon knew how to be of help. Their reputation for getting things done had spread through the wilderness, and so it was understandable that a British officer, Colonel Stevenson, should send them an urgent letter, explaining that he had hundreds of lost people on his hands. What to do?

On the day the runner brought the message, May 13, 1942, Father Stuart, the adventurer, told Father McAlindon to keep the work going at Kajihtu while he decided what could be done for the colonel. By foot he hurried the forty miles to Sumprabum to come upon utmost confusion.

Colonel Stevenson asked the priest to accept the responsibility for forty-nine refugees: twenty-five children from Bishop Strange Home, an orphanage operated by the Church of England in Rangoon; and seventeen adults, mostly women, who had seven children with them. All had come a thousand miles with the vague notion that this route across mountains and through jungles would take them to India. Now they were too exhausted to travel on. Colonel Stevenson said that he could give Father Stuart seventy bags of rice, some salt, a little cooking oil, and 3,000 rupees to take care of the forty-nine refugees, but when that was gone he would be on his own.

Getting them to Kajihtu would be a task. The children needed transportation, for most were too weak to walk the forty miles. By runner a note went to Father McAlindon asking for coolies to carry the children. When the coolies arrived they brought with them the monsoon, that season of torrential rain that pours two hundred inches of water on the Triangle. Suddenly rivers were too high to take the children across. The coolies waited around a few days, got bored, and left.

To hire more coolies Father Stuart returned to Kajihtu. How proud he was of his colleague: here the situation was just the opposite of that in Sumprabum. Father McAlindon had a knack for dialects, exuded confidence, and all in all had a way of bringing order out of chaos. As a Columban wrote: "He became the symbol of hope for all the tribes—as missionary, doctor, interpreter, pacifier, and food distributor. He won the hearts of all who came that way."

When word reached Kajihtu that retreating Chinese soldiers were in Sumprabum causing trouble, Father Stuart and the coolies hurried down the trail. A mile from Suprabum, Chinese soldiers arrested the missionary and made a show of marching him through town for an interview with their commanding officer. Since no interpreter could be found, the interview was postponed.

The refugees greeted the priest in near hysteria. The children were wailing and the adults displayed wild-eyed concern. Everyone spoke at once: the Chinese had looted the rice; soldiers had stolen clothes; an officer had fired a pistol through the bathroom door when children refused to unlock it.

Father Stuart found an interpreter and hurried to the commanding officer to make a plea for his refugees. The officer gave the priest a letter saying that the refugees were not to be molested and that the priest was allowed free passage in the Sumprabum area. The first time Father Stuart tried to use the letter a soldier tore it up and put him under armed guard with the refugees.

When four Kachin soldiers hiding in the jungle heard that Father Stuart and the refugees were starving, they went about collecting rice from villagers who had also lost food to the Chinese. To protect the precious parcel, the Kachins entered Sumprabum carrying three rifles and a shotgun.

The Chinese killed one of them; the other three returned the fire and killed four Chinese. When Father Stuart went to bury the dead man the Chinese opened fire on him, so he jumped into a ditch where the corpse sprawled, lay there until dark, and then crept out to complete the burial.

The three Kachin soldiers returned with reenforcements and killed twenty Chinese soldiers. This was enough to persuade the Chinese to move on.

Without warning in walked the Japanese. Father Stuart could have taken off into the jungle with the Kachin soldiers, but what about the refugees? He decided to stay and do some play-acting.

So as not to be suspected of spying, he took on the role of a naïve fellow, completely out of touch, hoping the Japanese would consider him harmless and so lose interest in him.

Right off he did the most naïve thing he could think of: he walked out into the middle of the road and stood there waiting for the Japanese major to approach on horseback.

"You Chinese?" the missionary asked.

The major spit and said, "Japanese!"

"You English?" asked the major.

The man from County Derry spit and said, "Irish!"

After dismounting, the major took a pistol in one hand and a sword in the other and began a deliberate inspection of the missionary. Slowly he circled him, making hissing sounds as he sucked air through his teeth.

"Where Irish?" he asked.

Father Stuart took the tall stick he carried, something of a shepherd's staff, and drew a circle in the clay.

"United States," he said.

Six feet away he drew another circle.

"England."

He was afraid to let Ireland appear too near either the United States or England, so he drew it in mid-Atlantic.

In the middle of the road the major held a long conference with his staff. After much sucking of air through the teeth, they decided that they could not remember declaring war on any Ireland.

A lieutenant who spoke English more fluently than the major asked Father Stuart what he knew about the war. Remembering that an American plane had flown over the day before, he decided to display more naïvete.

Pointing skyward he said, "Japanese plane, yesterday."

"How do you know?"

"White star."

The lieutenant asked why he thought a white star indicated a Japanese plane. Father Stuart pointed to the red star on the lieutenant's cap.

All the officers laughed. The lieutenant explained that the white star meant American. Japanese wear red stars.

With a puzzled look on his face, as though it was all very difficult, to comprehend, Father Stuart repeated, "White star American. Red star, Japanese."

After the officers decided that this simple soul was harmless enough, the lieutenant admitted to the priest that he was a Christian, having attended a Baptist school before the war. Each evening the young officer came to the refugee camp and took part in singing hymns.

While searching the refugee quarters, the lieutenant came upon a British radio transmitter hidden in a closet of the women's section. Fortunately, the wires were cut and showed signs of rust indicating that the equipment had been abandoned months earlier by fleeing British soldiers.

"I assured the lieutenant that I didn't even know it was there," wrote Father Stuart. "He looked at the set for some time and then looked at my face for some time in silence. I was feeling uneasy. Finally he took the set, walked to the edge of the compound, and threw it over. It rolled down a rather steep slope into the jungle below. Turning to me the Jap officer remarked, 'My major won't even bother to look down there.' "

Fathers Stuart and McAlindon, half starved and filled with fever, worked themselves to a state of exhaustion in finding enough rice to keep the refugees alive. Finally they collected enough coolies and elephants to help the women and children on their way. On October 2, 1942, the refugees took off from Sumprabum for Fort Hertz up near the Himalayas. From there they would be taken by air to India.

By now Fathers Stuart and McAlindon looked so wraithlike that a British officer ordered them to India for rest and medical attention. Hardly had their plane landed when the two of them began pulling strings for a return trip. Absolutely not, said Major General Pearce, the chief of civil affairs for Burma, adding that since the priests had done so much for the government they would have quarters in India for the duration.

Just as it looked as though the British general would have his way, the missionaries were offered a return trip under the auspices of a hush-hush outfit, a group of Americans who called themselves Detachment 101. It was a unit of the Office of Strategic Services (OSS) dedicated to espionage and sabotage.

When the OSS first entered the lives of the two priests, they were startled by the bizarre outfit. They thought the secret agents were pulling their legs in telling outrageous stories about their training program. In time, though, the Columbans were tempted to believe that many of the OSS instructors in the States really were selected from among the nation's top criminals. Who could better teach someone how to crack a safe, pick a pocket, or forge a document than men who had spent their lives perfecting such talents? One forgery instructor was so proficient that after an officer had autographed a piece of paper, the forger would imitate it with such skill on two identical pieces of paper that the odds were in his favor when betting five dollars that the officer would not identify his own signature.

Before entering Burma, the OSS trained at a remote place in India called Nazera where instructors worked hard to teach agents hand-to-hand combat, Morse code, map-reading, cryptography, and silent ways to kill a sentry.

The OSS dropped agents behind Japanese lines to open a base with the code name of Knothead. There natives built an airstrip of sorts—on a slant and somewhat curved—and placed portable huts on it to give the appearance of a village. When a plane wanted to land, natives hurriedly carried off the huts only to replace them, like stage scenery, after the plane's departure.

One of the things the OSS did was to help rescue pilots shot down on the flight across "the Hump." Colonel Carl Eifler, commanding officer of Detachment 101, OSS, saw right off that Kachins, with their knowledge of the wilderness, were ideal for such work, and since his agents had reported how much the Kachins respected Fathers Stuart and McAlindon, he was interested in meeting them. It was evident that the Columbans were men who could get things done, and so the colonel began adding burdens to the many that already weighted them down.

Colonel Eifler explained to the priests that the Hump flight was organized because Burma, the wedge between India and China, was now held by the Japanese. As though they didn't know! To get supplies from India to China, planes flew across the Himalayas where northern Burma penetrates Tibet. On the treacherous route, peaks thrust upward to more than 24,000 feet above sea level. Flight distance was anywhere from 500 to 1,000 miles depending on which airstrips were used of the thirteen in India and the four in China.

In the course of the war, about 900 planes went down on the Hump. Some the victims of Japanese zeros; many the victims of storms and overworked equipment. No one will ever know how many went down because of terrible fatigue. A pilot who cracked under the strain was spoken of as "Hump happy." Fortunately the Kachins saved about 700 of the crews.

One lieutenant parachuted into the jungle to find a pair of Oriental eyes peering at him through the thicket. Thinking it was a Japanese he took off down the trail, ran up and down a couple of hills and through a few streams before collapsing from exhaustion. Hardly had he sprawled upon the ground than the Oriental eyes were there. A hand thrust a note at him, one written in English by Father McAlindon: "Follow me, I am a friend."

Father Stuart found an American fighter pilot tangled on a tree limb sixty feet up in the air. He yelled, "Drop your parachute!" When the 'chute hit the ground, the priest unzipped the pocket containing emergency rations and calmly sat down beneath a tree to enjoy a rare treat—real chocolate.

Up among the branches the American began to fume and shout. "Be patient, lad, be patient," admonished the priest, and added, "My Kachins will be along to get you down. Unless the Japanese hear you shouting and get here first."

Then it dawned on the pilot. "Are you Father Stuart?" The priest answered, "Who else would be stupid enough to be in this part of the world?"

Refugees once more became Father Stuart's burden when he was asked to lead 241 of them—mostly women, children, and old men—on a 21-day trek in January of 1944. Rain fell almost incessantly, starvation was always present, and the Japanese were near. Father Stuart's notes are filled with sentences that touch the heart.

In describing the events of January 29, he wrote: "It was a hard journey and about five miles of it meant wading upstream in a knee-deep river. It was very difficult for the children and for the blind women who were in our party. There were heavy thunderstorms and everybody felt very cold, both with being wet through and with wading in ice-cold waters. We came upon a village that had been deserted over a year ago and wild elephants had knocked down all the houses. All put up temporary shelters. There was no rice available. Our patrols went out in search of game, or even buffalo left behind by villagers, but had no success. Some of the refugees were sick and some had developed sore feet in addition to swollen joints."

The refugees began to feel safe in Naw Bum when an American unit, Merrill's Marauders, came along the trail. General Frank Merrill's mission was to clear the Japanese out of upper Burma, yard by yard, while American engineers on bulldozers cut the Ledo Road through the jungle from India to China. This eventually allowed trucks to carry supplies to China, a supplement to those being flown across the Hump.

When Father Stuart went up the trail to meet the Marauders, an officer pointed to Myitkyina on the map and asked how to pronounce it. Father Stuart said, "In America what you call playing hookey from school, in Ireland we call 'mitchin.' So you just remember that word, hit it hard, and add 'naw.' Mitchin-naw."

But not even Father Stuart realized that day, March 15, 1944, how far away Myitkyina really was. It would take lots of bloodshed and five months of time before the town would be free of Japanese.

"When the men found out I was a Catholic priest, quite a number were very anxious for me to go to their bivouac area to hear confessions. They had then no Catholic chaplain with them. I spent all that evening and most of the night hearing confessions of the men of Col. McGee's B Battalion. One man came to be baptized. His two buddies had taught him all the necessary doctrine and he was very keen to be received into the Church. I baptized him on the banks of the Tanai Hka at midnight. I was very glad to have been able to help these men because the battalion was later surrounded by Japanese and besieged in a Kachin village for thirteen days. Many of the boys who came to me that night lie buried there."

The Marauders were jinxed. Things were always going from bad to worse. Father Stuart wrote: "The men were in very bad shape. B Battalion had marched for twelve hours the previous day to get through Warong before they could be cut off. They had very little food and got no sleep. They had come from Auche to Nhpum at the double and had suffered casualties. Some of the men were still shocked and jittery. Some of these, when they found I was there, sought me out for a few quiet confidences. It relieved them to have someone to speak to who had time to listen to them and who didn't try to explain to them with trembling voice and shaking knees that there was nothing to fear. I was as afraid as they were but I kept my mouth shut. Weeks later in Assam, some of these men, perfectly cured, came and thanked me for giving them confidence that morning."

Whenever a soldier began speaking with bitterness, Father Stuart had a way of saying something that would relieve the tension. When one of them began complaining that he had been in the jungle for eighteen months without leave, the missionary said, "In my branch of the service we come over for 120 months without leave. Of course it's worth it. Our reward is that we get sent to Ireland!"

Father Stuart did so many favors for the military that the military was pleased when it could do something for him. Colonel Peers, the new commander of the OSS unit, was delighted when he could send a radio message into the jungle saying that Father Stuart's brother was in India. A light plane flew the missionary to Nazira where he spent a few days with Staff Sergeant Frank Stuart. The brothers had not seen each other since that day twenty-one years earlier when Frank had left Ireland for Canada.

Back in the jungle, the missionary felt he was doing what he was meant to do: "I had Mass at the airstrip this Easter morning. Many Americans attended. There was general rejoicing when word came in that C Battalion had forced their way through to Nhpum. Arrangements were made for the immediate evacuation of the wounded from B Battalion, who were reported to be on their way down to the airstrip. Some of these men had been wounded twelve days ago. They were reported to have had 115 wounded and 29 killed while they were besieged in Nhpum. All the battalions were tired and emaciated. In addition to wounded, many had dysentery and some were suffering from war neurosis."

General Merrill kept the ubiquitous James Stuart near his headquarters as much as possible. He saw that the priest and the Kachins had great rapport and that the Kachins were the best fighters in Burma. Shortly before his own death, General Merrill wrote, "Father Stuart was the bravest man I ever met."

For helping save refugees Father Stuart was appointed an officer of the Most Excellent Order of the British Empire. Later the United States War Department awarded him the Medal of Freedom for his work with the Office of Strategic Services and with Merrill's Marauders.

At the end of the war an OSS agent asked Father Stuart to write a report of his experiences, which he did. In the final paragraph he said:

"Father McAlindon has had a more exciting time than I had but he was not so fortunate in his publicity agents. Colonel Eifler once confided to me that at the beginning the OSS didn't want me at all. They wanted Father Mac but they took me too to make sure of getting Father Mac. Later he said that—well, that I had a certain publicity value. You should ask Father Mac to give you some facts of his life during the war years, for publicity purposes. I don't think you will succeed, but at any rate you will get a lesson in real humility to counteract this egotistical report of mine."

Fourteen

DEATH IN MANDALAY

When the Japanese commanding officer in Bhamo told Monsignor Usher to take his Columbans to Mandalay for internment, he remarked in passing that they would have to pay their own expenses to get there. To make the situation more dreary he assigned them to an unsafe riverboat so tiny that nineteen priests and six native helpers had to exist in a deck space of eighteen by twelve feet.

"Should you wish to take a little exercise," Father Rillstone wrote, "you could do this by alternately sitting and standing briskly. A sudden movement of the arms would almost certainly elicit a cry of protest. The rest of the deck was equally crowded, the space being taken by various groups of Indians and Burmese, whole families of them—men, women, and children."

The rule that prevailed at night was that no one was permitted to turn in his sleep or lie on his back for there was not enough room. To remain in one position was especially penitential because of the rivets in the sheet metal deck covering.

The journey down the Irrawaddy from Bhamo to Mandalay should have taken at most three or four days, but instead it took twelve, with rain pouring down much of the time. Several days were spent stranded on sand bars, and had not the Columbans manned the windlass to help an incompetent crew, the journey would have dragged out much longer.

As the boat approached the dock at Mandalay, the priests came upon a scene of such desolation that they flinched at the sight of it. They remembered the Mandalay of a few years earlier, and now all was chaotic rubble as far as the horizon.

Perhaps no city was ever more thoroughly burned. When the Japanese approached and the British fled, early in 1942, the town burned without ceasing for three weeks. Bombs from Japanese planes started the holocaust and a wind off the Irrawaddy spread the flames. To any area that seemed spared, anarchists applied torches with thoroughness. Each darkness brought visions of the world's last night.

In *Retreat with Stilwell,* Jack Belden wrote: "When it appeared as if there was nothing more to burn, flames curiously burst out of the already devastated portion of the metropolis and separate bonfires sprang up on every street. For twenty-one days the destruction had continued, until Mandalay was no longer a city, but a field of tile and charcoal. The bazaars, the railway station, the schools, the hospitals, foreign churches, and Buddhist temples; in fact, every house, shop, market place, and building had vanished. Yet miraculously the flames continued to find something to feed on and the fire never died out."

The Columbans were surprised to see that in the midst of charred ruins there was one sector untouched: the palace and grounds of the kings of Burma, set in the heart of Mandalay, girded around by a moat and fenced in by a red brick wall. The Japanese had never bombed it, and the arsonists had left it alone. But its days were numbered.

Not a Japanese soldier was at the dock to meet the "prisoners." So they loaded their effects onto bullock carts for a cheerless three-mile trek to the military headquarters, where they were told that they should have reported to the civil authorities a mile back. There one of the civil authorities said, "No, you are a military problem."

At this point Monsignor Usher told his military problems to loll beside the road while he and Father Murphy returned to headquarters. After much to-do the military accepted the responsibility and gave the two priests a lorry to transport the missionaries and their belongings to a fine house at Mandalay Agricultural College well outside the city. What a luxury, to lie on a wooden floor and stretch and turn at will— after that sheet metal deck.

The house, however, was surrounded by Japanese units and so attracted the attention of allied bombers. Drums of gasoline stored all about did not contribute to peace of mind, as day after day and night after night, the prisoners endured air raids.

Monsignor Usher thought that if the Japanese were going to keep them in custody they would surely feed them. Not so. The military would not even consider selling rice at controlled prices.

"Luckily we had about 10,000 rupees and prices were fairly normal at the time," Father Howe wrote in a letter at the end of the war. "We carried on without much difficulty until we got our first money from

Ireland in August. It wasn't a day too soon. Not long after, Monsignor Usher received an inquiry from Father John Dooley, our procurator in Rome, about our financial condition.

"Sometime in January the attitude of the Japanese changed and we were allowed to move out of the compound and go around the town. We had as much freedom of movement as anyone in Mandalay. It was a concession which we knew better than to use overmuch."

Monsignor Usher felt concern about the fate of Father E. J. McCarthy, the former superior of the Columbans in the United States. When war reached Burma and the British army was on the run, Father McCarthy was at Maymyo, a hill station in the south, recovering from an illness. Three weeks before the fall of Bhamo, Father McCarthy had written:

"My days here are crowded. The alerts usually go during the afternoon and we have to go to the trenches. Not that we have had many bombing raids, but the few we have had were pretty terrible. The last one, a week ago, left a trail of destruction across the town.

"My afternoons are taken up with the casualties in the hospitals. As I am the only English-speaking priest in the town, the work of attending to the wounded soldiers naturally came my way. I am very glad that I happened to be here.

"The wounded are brought up the Irrawaddy in hospital boats and then transferred to the train at Mandalay and brought here to Maymyo. Now that Mandalay has been burned and transportation disorganized these poor fellows have undergone a great deal by the time they arrive here. Some of them have been as long as twenty-seven days en route."

A year passed and then all of a sudden there stood Father McCarthy in Mandalay. The Columbans were delighted to see him. With him was Father Cooney, cut off on his way back to Bhamo from Toungoo where he had been helping at a mission. The Japanese high command at Maymyo had allowed them to continue caring for refugees for a year before deciding to send them along to Mandalay.

In October of 1943 the Japanese said that they wanted to occupy the house and so the Columbans would have to move to St. John's Leper Asylum. The missionaries did not know at the time that Bishop Faliere was using his influence to have them transferred to the asylum where he had been living since the destruction of his cathedral and house.

In writing of the 300 lepers that the Columbans would be with, Father Rillstone said: "This may sound a little unpleasant. In Burma you become accustomed to the sight of leprosy. Many of the street beggars are lepers. Much of the money you handle will already have been handled by lepers. Some of the people you shake hands with will be lepers. The thought of this is a little repugnant at first, but once you know something about the disease it becomes easy. As long as there are no open sores it is quite safe, but should you have any cuts or scratches, it could be dangerous to handle anything used by a leper."

The Columbans thought that since they were no longer in a military camp they would be free from air raids. The leper asylum got its share, however. In one twenty-four-hour period they absorbed thirteen raids. The place was nearly destroyed by a lone bomber on a pitch-black night. Somehow Major Brown of the U.S. Air Corps learned about the prisoners in the asylum. He and a former Baptist missionary, Captain Cummings, passed the word along to the pilots, and from that day on no bombs fell within a mile of the leper asylum.

During the seventeen months in St. John's, the internees maintained their sanity by keeping busy. Nuns, about a hundred of them, repaired the clothing; and priests kept the shoes somewhat intact.

"All told," said John Howe, "we repaired hundreds of pairs of shoes, some of which were almost completely worn through when we got them. In the end we became so skilled that we were able to turn out new pairs for Fathers McGonagle and Doody."

Gathering firewood also kept them occupied. Of this Lawrence Mc-Mahon wrote: "It took a war to make me realize the latent talents of my confreres. I was even surprised at my own ability with a crosscut saw. When I made my bashful debut I was prepared for criticism from my more expert brethern. But no; apparently I was a 'natural,' with even stroke and superb timing; at least that is what I was told. At any rate we succeeded, by our own efforts, in securing from the bombed trees around Mandalay enough firewood to last us for the whole period of our internment."

Baking bread is an activity that John Howe remembers: "Bread could be bought in Mandalay, but it was of poor quality and eventually became too dear. Europeans compelled to live on rice alone are exposed to the danger of beriberi, and so when bread became too expensive, and our funds were running out, we invested most of what we had left in flour and began experimenting in baking. Eventually we succeeded, and turned out as fine a bread as one could hope to have with inferior flour. It was hard work. In the tropics you have to give yeast bread a terrific pounding with the fists in order to make it rise. We usually took turns at the pounding in shifts of two, and you can imagine the amount of perspiration that got mixed up with the dough in the course of a half hour."

Then there were the hens, ducks, pigs, and a cow to be looked after. This meant more than feeding them; houses had to be put up. The Columbans went around town searching out half-burned nails, bamboo matting, and poles. Fathers McEvoy and Barry did most of the carpentry.

The Burmese had difficulty with Irish names, and so they referred to the priests as "the Father who looks after the hens," and "the Father who looks after the cow."

The cow was the focus of much concern and discussion. Milk was scarce and the small amount available each day was highly watered. When some of the priests fell ill, more milk was needed. The milkman said the only way he could supply more would be to add more water to the daily quota.

"After much deliberation," said Father McMahon, "it was decided to purchase a cow. It was a serious undertaking, because the initial expense of the animal, plus its upkeep, would be a heavy strain on our limited resources.

"Eventually the cow was bought, and a fine animal she was. Even my inexperienced eye could see that. Not that I had anything to do with the selection. I had seen cows grazing in fields, and once I had spent a week on a farm. As a native of Chicago I had visited the stockyards and seen all kinds of steers there. But these were not qualifications to fit me for the present business, and so I was not a member of the board of directors who bought the cow."

When the cow arrived and gave no milk the board of directors patiently explained to the priest from Chicago that milk would be plentiful after the cow had had her calf. When asked when that event would occur, the members of the board looked wise and mentioned a date in the not-too-distant future.

"Never did a cow receive more attention," said Father McMahon. "Considering that there was a war on, her diet was such as to excite envy among the bovine population of the neighborhood. But the days and weeks passed and still there was no calf. The experts were hard put to answer questions from those of us who had not had the happy privilege of spending our youth on a farm. In fact the episode of the cow is one of those incidents which our experts are still unwilling to discuss. It is true that the calf finally arrived—but only after the liberation of Mandalay when the milk problem was no longer serious."

When it came to preparing a gigantic garden, Monsignor Usher did most of the rough work. He and several other Columbans also kept busy with some intellectual projects. As he said later, "We studied and wrote in various languages."

The monsignor's major work was writing a history of the Catholic Church in Burma, based on copious notes Father E. J. McCarthy had collected. Since he knew his supply of paper was limited, he wrote in an exceedingly cramped hand, crowding as much as possible onto a page until the manuscript reached about 40,000 words.

The first paragraph begins: "There were Christians in the Tartar-Chinese army which invaded Burma in 1287. Traces of them are found at Pagan. Near the earliest of the great temples there is a shrine called the Cave of Kyanzittha. A fresco on its walls exhibits eight crosses, four Latin and four Greek, distributed on the eight petals of a lotus around a cross in the centre. The same design appears in frescoes in the Roman catacombs. The artist meant to represent crosses of wood since he was careful to imitate its fibers and knots. There were many Nestorian Christians from Turkestan in the employ of the conqueror, Kublai Khan."

Father Way used his time to prepare two catechisms, one for small children, and one for adults, both would eventually be printed in Calcutta. The catechism that he had inherited from the French Missionaries was too advanced for the very young and not advanced enough for an older group.

While in Mandalay, Father Way learned to read music and play the organ, instructed by two nuns who were music teachers. These courses were helpful through the years when he taught in a school for catechists. He later said, "The internment in Mandalay was a tremendous help for the work I was to perform from 1947 onward."

Illness, especially mysterious fevers, became an accepted part of life. The great dread, though, was a toothache, for there was no dentist available. One day Father Rillstone suffered such an agonizing ache that he borrowed a forceps from the dispensary, handed it to Father McEvoy, sat in a chair, gripped the rungs, and said, go ahead.

"He had never pulled a tooth before," recalled Father Rillstone, "and

I never had a tooth pulled in this way, so that evened things up a bit. It would be a new experience for both of us. At first attempt the forceps slipped. This seemed to arouse the fighting blood in Father McEvoy. He got another grip on the offending tooth and said, 'By the Lord Harry it'll come out this time or else!' Luckily for me it wasn't the 'or else.' "

The most nerve-racking days came as the war drew to a close. When the British were moving in to recapture Mandalay, the Japanese placed a big gun in front of the leper asylum, and, of course, the British fired back.

The strain began to tell. Everyone became visibly more gaunt. Day or night there was hardly a moment free from the sound of shells and machine guns, mortars and hand grenades.

Suddenly on March 15, 1945, came the electrifying news that a British unit had dug in at the corner of the asylum grounds. Within minutes the soldiers were passing out chocolates and cigarettes.

During the three-and-a-half years of war, each Columban had become familiar with the face of death. All had somehow survived until now in the closing hours.

While Father Thomas Murphy was saying Mass on the morning of March 16, 1945, a stray Japanese shell burst above the room used as a chapel, tore the top off the tabernacle, pierced the Mass book, and penetrated the altar table. Of the twelve priests in the room, several were injured but none so severely as Father Murphy.

"I heard some groans and in the cloud of dust saw sombeody being carried outside," wrote Father Howe a few days later. "It was Father Jim Devine. His face was covered with blood and he seemed to be badly wounded. Father McCarthy gave him absolution and Father Tom Walsh and I carried him to the shelter. On the way, Tom said he thought he had got a touch of the shell himself. He certainly had: a large gash on the shoulder, another on the arm, and some lesser ones.

"Then Father Dan Cooney came along and said that Father Tom Murphy had been badly wounded. One foot was mangled and the other also injured. We carried him to the dispensary in the main building, where there was consternation and tears among the sisters as they saw priest after priest carried in bleeding. But they did a great job and in a short time everybody had been fixed up except Tom Murphy, who was obviously a case for expert attention. In addition to the leg wounds he had also been severely injured in the stomach."

Only major surgery would save his life, but no one at the asylum was skilled enough to perform it. Father McEvoy, who had shown exceptional courage time and again, volunteered to go for help. Cautiously, he slipped out the back and waded through a canal to reach the British outpost. The officer-in-charge sent a radio message to headquarters for help; headquarters promised that if necessary they would fly Father Murphy to India within two hours.

As Father Howe recalled, "When we gave him the last sacraments, I think he knew it was the end. As he was being carried out and we said our goodbyes, he begged pardon for his faults and promised us his prayers."

Since the victim was in such a critical condition, Father McEvoy and his fellow stretcher bearers decided not to take the back route but to save time by going down the main road. The Japanese held their fire and the group arrived safely at the outpost. A gun carrier was waiting to transport the victim a few miles to an ambulance. Every care was taken, but before the ambulance could reach the field hospital Father Murphy was dead.

When the stretcher bearers returned, they brought news that the British would send trucks for any of the prisoners who could reach an assembly point three miles away. Bishop Faliere and several sisters said they would stay behind to care for the lepers but that everyone else should go. Father McMahon and Monsignor Usher said they would remain a day longer until two local priests arrived from the other side of Mandalay.

The trucks could not come close to the leper asylum because they would have been shelled by the Japanese. So the missionaries and other internees, about 160 in all, slipped out the back way, sloshed through a canal and moved along a remote road in uneasy procession—a nun with a broken leg, several patients so weakened by fever that they had to be carried, and a few priests hobbling along with pieces of shrapnel in their legs. On his back Father Edmund McGovern carried a French bishop, age eighty. In spite of all the pain, they moved with spirit. Had it not been for Father Murphy's death it would have been a glorious St. Patrick's Day.

Fifteen

BUT NOT WEEPING

"Well, it is all over," wrote Monsignor Usher, "and God has been good to us. We lost only one priest when we might have lost a couple of dozen.

"Among the ashes of our buildings we sit, but not weeping."

The first priests back to Bhamo were in for a shock. Father Thomas McEvoy wrote: "The old Bhamo has ceased to be. Not a house is standing. Everywhere there are trenches, shell holes, bomb craters. The District Commissioner, a Colonel Byrne, received us very kindly, and put us up in his own place, not in Bhamo but in a village about two miles out. This will serve as 'Bhamo' until the old town can be rebuilt."

In Katha and Myitkyina all buildings were gone. At Meinhkat mission buildings were destroyed along with the whole village and most of the people. At Hpunpyen, a hill station, nothing remained of mission property. The buildings at Zaubung were burned with the village. Most outpost stations had ceased to exist.

Here and there were a few happy surprises. Father McEvoy, dreading to think of what might have happened to Panghkak, returned to find that except for some looting everything was much the same.

"We lost four of our five cows and some ponies. I am so glad to see the rest of the property safe that I do not worry about the stolen livestock."

Father Bernard Way was also delighted with his homecoming. Shortly after returning to Bhamo in May of 1945, he set off with a Mass kit on his back and a few supplies for his old parish at Ting Sing. On the way he stopped at the village of Lailaw where he had left about 200 Catholics.

"Our arrival caused great jubilation. The whole village came along, and the people were so manifestly overjoyed to see us again that I felt deeply moved. Next day we had a big feast, and what with baptisms, blessings, and interviews of all kinds, it was a busy time. And so with all the other villages.

"I had dreaded coming back to find many fallen again into the worship of spirits; I found, instead, that the majority had remained firm, despite suffering, war, the absence of priests, and even of teachers, for three years. In Lailaw there had actually been an increase in the number of people anxious to become Christians, and last year they had built a new bamboo chapel. I had thirty-five adult baptisms followed by first communions. Monsignor Usher confirmed these new Catholics a few weeks later."

In Ting Sing, the central village of his parish, Father Way found that some of the mission outbuildings had been destroyed for firewood, but the people had preserved most of the movable things. Whenever an alarm was given, the Ting Sing Catholics would make for the jungle carrying vestments, chalice, monstrance, books, and especially the band instruments of which they were so proud. It was heavy work, but they hesitated to leave things in the jungle permanently because of storms and the ever-present ants. When the danger was passed temporarily, back came the things into Ting Sing. With each new crisis the work had to be done all over again.

"My property had a high priority on their list of things to evacuate. They ran the risk of losing their own possessions in an attempt to save mine. I lost some books, school equipment, pots, and blankets, but when you consider that we emerged from the turmoil with tried and trustworthy Catholics the losses are not worth a moment's thought."

At the time, Monsignor Usher wrote: "The priests are overjoyed with the steadiness of the Catholics during our separation from them. With comparatively few defectors we find the main body with a more lively faith than when last we saw them."

He told a story that illustrates this spiritual growth: In a remote village, first reached by the Columbans in 1938, all the families were relatives of one old patriarch "to whom the faith was a gift direct and lavish." In 1944 the Japanese, by way of vengeance for something the Kachin Levies had done, surrounded the village and massacred everyone in it. The patriarch and a few others happened to be absent at the time. Instead of seeking ways for revenge, the Kachin way of doing things through the centuries, the old patriarch prayed for the dead.

When Father Stuart met the old man he was touched by the story because a year earlier he himself had been caught up in a show of Kachin vengeance. A friend of his, Lazum Tu, had been attacked by two hired killers who bungled the job. The missionary bandaged the victim and cared for him until he died a few hours later. When neighbors came to the basha to build a coffin, bullets began penetrating the bamboo walls.

"I threw myself flat on the floor," said Father Stuart, "and then all hell broke loose. About thirty Kachins armed with Kachin muskets and British and Chinese rifles were firing on the house. I think they hadn't intended to kill anybody then, merely to put us out of the house; but quite a number of shots passed through the house, and a slug tore through the back of the cane chair on which I had been sitting."

Lazum Tu had died without knowing why. Father Stuart learned that years earlier a boy had been accidentally shot and a Kachin, Kauri Ladoi, the government representative for the Triangle when Father Stuart first went to Kajihtu, had given the boy's father 500 rupees in compensation when the father expected a thousand. For this, Kauri Ladoi was marked for assassination. However, since he had died of cholera years earlier, someone else would have to pay the price. Lazum Tu was selected to pay for the ancient bitterness because his wife was a niece of Kauri Ladoi.

In less dramatic ways all the Columbans found the spiritual lives of their parishioners strengthened by war. Father McEvoy wrote: "I have spent the last three weeks touring the hills to see my parishioners, and was delighted to find that in most places not only was there no decrease in the number of Catholics, there was actually an increase. My tour was rather widespread; I must have covered a few hundred miles in all.

"In each village the Catholics were so glad to meet the priest again that usually they stayed up most of the night chatting about events of the last three years. Three weeks of this kind of thing left me rather sleepy. On the way back to Panghkak I nearly fell off the pony a few times. I simply couldn't keep awake."

Even with all of the losses of property, Monsignor Usher wrote with optimism to his superior general: "Prospects in the Bhamo prefecture are brighter than before. Father Stuart, in his three years of wandering throughout the northern portions of the prefecture while we were interned, has made a host of friends among the people up there. I think we shall have to apply to you for a dozen more priests when we have fully explored possibilities for the future.

"I cannot exaggerate our debt of gratitude to the Paris Foreign Missionaries for their help and kindness toward us during these past years. Bishop Faliere housed us during our stay in Mandalay and put everything he had at our disposal. Fathers Kelleher and Cloonan experienced the same kindness from Bishop Provost and his priests in Rangoon."

The Columbans were not long back at their missions when they lost another confrere. Father Thomas Walsh, one of the pioneers of 1936, died of malaria on December 13, 1945.

A few weeks earlier he had suffered an attack in his mission station in the jungle. After nine days of illness he decided to try to reach a Bhamo hospital, sixty miles away. Kachins carried him on a bamboo stretcher to the foot of the hill; a bullock cart was to take him the rest of the way.

Two American soldiers, attached to the army's Cemeteries' Department, happened to come along in a truck. Hearing of the priest's plight they went to a great deal of trouble to get to him and to take him to the hospital. There they subscribed a substantial sum which they said they hoped would be of help in his work.

When Father Walsh died a few days later, Monsignor Usher wrote to Columban Headquarters in Omaha:

"His death is a terrible blow to us. Each of us has lost a friend to whom we were bound by something a great deal deeper than the ordinary ties of comradeship. The foundation of it was his complete unselfishness. In a difficult and lonely mission he never showed that he gave his troubles and hardships a thought. When he met any of the rest of us he was full of jokes and good humor in his quiet, gentle way, and none of them ever at the expense of anyone else.

"As a missionary he was one of the very best. He had a great gift for languages, but his proficiency in them was more than a gift. He never ceased trying to improve. As soon as he got hold of a phrase he tried it out on all he met, repeating it over and over to get the right tone and twisting it this way and that to test the exact shade of meaning. The language of his parish was Kachin. He thought it so habitually that he spoke in it almost all the time during his last illness. His people had a great affection for him. They could hardly help it, for they were only returning in some measure the ardent affection which he had for them. He was as simple in his ways as they and entered into all their joys and sorrows. There will be many a sad heart among them when they learn that they will see him no more."

The way the Columbans accepted any loss without feeling sorry for themselves made a favorable impression on American servicemen. An air force colonel, Roland H. Cipolla, wrote:

"They were nothing more than skin and bones and in many cases disease-ridden, but they could still joke and smile. And the strangest thing of all, they did everything within their power to try to help us whenever possible.

"They should have had a year's recuperation leave by ordinary standards. Instead, when I invited Father McGonagle to spend a leave with me he said, "Thanks, no. I have several families of Kachins in the hills. I must get back.""

How a sense of humor persisted in spite of monsoons, malaria, typhus, and other difficulties was something else the Americans remembered. Colonel Cipolla told of asking several missionaries to dinner at Company B, 1975th Aviation Engineers when they were on their way to various villages. Father McGonagle said grace before the meal: "Thank God for these offerings and thank God that the Monsignor doesn't see us all here together."

The generosity of the Columbans was something else that impressed all who met them. Through the years Colonel Cipolla remembered a gift from Father McGonagle:

"Just before the Japanese captured him in 1942, he buried his meager belongings in the jungle. After the war he traveled on foot the day and the night before he reached here, and all he had with him was a little sack strapped to his back with some rice, hard tack, and some tea. It had been raining incessantly, and he was drenched to the skin and covered with jungle leeches. In his shirt he had tucked away a fifth of Johnny Walker whiskey that he had buried three years earlier. He said upon greeting me, 'I thought you would like this.' Certainly, if anyone needed Johnny Walker that day it was Father McGonagle. But he just had to show his appreciation."

In a long conversation with Monsignor Usher, the colonel learned of the work the Columbans had started in Burma six years before war reached those hills.

"It was a surprise to me that they were not primarily concerned with counting converts. Their main objective was to elevate the Shans and

Kachins so that they, in turn, could spread a doctrine of spiritual democracy, freedom, and a better way of life.

"Monsignor Usher told me: 'If you believe strongly enough in your accomplishments and if you pursue them with honesty and conviction, God will do the rest.' "

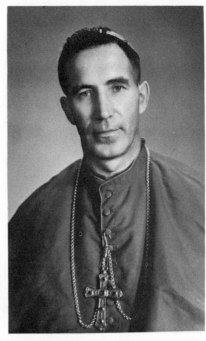

Bishop Paul Grawng,
first Kachin bishop.

Bishop Howe.

Archbishop Knox, Bishop Howe, and Father O'Connor
pray at Monsignor Usher's grave in Bhamo.

Father James Stuart.

Sisters Bernadine and Josepha talk with their taxi driver.

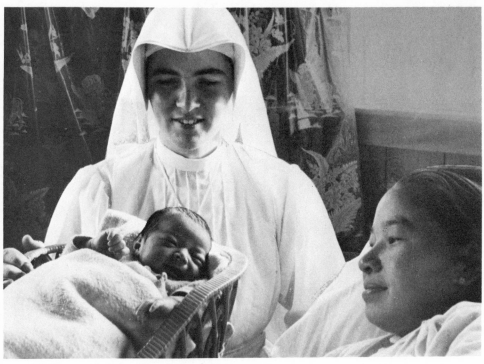

Mother and baby at clinic in Manbang.

Father Rillstone and friend.

Bishops Grawng and Howe.

Father Stuart and General Merrill receive gifts from Kachin tribesman.

Christmas dinner in Sinlum.

A typical scene in Bhamo bazaar.

Leaders of victory dance carry crosses.

Kachins are a rugged people.

Shan mother.

Kachin mother.

Three generations of Kachins.

One form of transportation in upper Burma.

Huge Burmese idol looms above the wreckage of Bhamo.

Traditional Kachin flute.

Burmese children.

Boy rings church bell—a defused navy bomb!

Sister Benedicta
and Bhamo pupil.

Father Rillstone at Bhamo school.

Confirmation ceremony choir.

Little Indian girl.

Girl from Sinlum.

A Karens girl in Sisters' school in Bhamo.

Little Chinese boy.

Little scholar of the Buddhist monks' school.

Shan festival play.

Art of weaving is known by every Kachin girl.

Girl in typical Kachin dress.

Kachin girl and her brother.

Sixteen

NEW ARRIVALS

Monsignor Usher was still impatient to be up and doing, and yet war had taught him something about mortality and its limitations. "You must be content with a very limited degree of success in your lifetime," he wrote. "Be satisfied with the less congenial work of clearing the ground and winning from it the first thin returns. For the later workers is reserved the happier task of gathering the rich harvest."

Whether or not he was aware of it, this was the attitude of his patron, the great Patrick: The saint, so it is said, accepted both the gains and losses of life with equal gratitude because of his unshaken hope in the promises of Providence.

Such an outlook was too mature for the dozen young priests on their way to Burma; they would have to grow toward it with the years. Since they lacked the lessons of war, and those of accumulated experience, their hearts would sink, as Patrick Usher's had when first he saw Bhamo. Unfortunately, the monsignor would not be there to greet them; he was in Ireland chafing under the doctor's orders for a prolonged rest.

One of the new priests, Daniel Treanor, wrote: "On a late Sunday evening in September of 1946 we disembarked at Rangoon full of enthusiasm as we took our first steps on the soil of Burma. The land and the people must have been awaiting our arrival for the Good News."

Suddenly they were struck by the shabbiness of it all! The war had been over for a year but everything was still seedy and impermanent. The sadness of the transient, the rootless, hung heavy in the air. Father Treanor continued: "There our ardour died, *veni, vidi*—but we had no return ticket."

Father James Fisher, a Columban from Dublin, met the dispirited young men and helped ease their way through a warren of inconveniences. The old China hand, now a military chaplain, accompanied the new missionaries on the long, cheerless journey to Mandalay, where Bishop Faliere welcomed them with his usual graciousness.

At supper, as the bishop told of his loss of cathedral, clergy house, convents, and schools, the little that was left to him was suddenly threatened: The room heaved like a ship at sea and the furniture did a grotesque dance. Although the visitors had seen nothing like this before, their instincts told them that the safest place was outside.

One of the Columbans wrote: "Fortunately, in a few minutes the earthquake was over and the ground resumed its firm and sober habit."

The bishop spoke of how Burma feels earthquakes at intervals of ten or fifteen years, but none of catastrophic proportions. In about 1912 an unusually severe one at Mandalay damaged the cathedral belfry and smashed the dome over the leper asylum chapel. A milder one in 1934 did considerable damage in southern Burma.

"The ordinary houses and most of the churches are of wood or wood framing," said the bishop, "and so are never in great danger. The joints of the timber yield with the movements of the earth and the worst that happens is that pictures fall from the walls."

The Columbans used to make the trip from Mandalay to Bhamo by railroad or river, but during the war the roadbed and bridges were blown and the steamboats sunk. So through the help of Father Fisher and a Colonel McCarthy the young priests traveled the last 375 miles by truck.

They were told that transportation in Burma was in a state of transition. Ponies were still needed, but not as much as before, now that the Ledo Road ran diagonally across the Columban territory.

Castoff army vehicles brought new possibilities for getting around. An army colonel warned a Columban against buying a used army truck. "They drive the guts out of them, and then put in a requisition for a new one."

One of the older Columbans told the young missionaries, "A castoff jeep always makes you into a man of parts, all sorts of parts. Surrounded by boxes of nuts and bolts you spend hours selecting and discarding. Finally you find a piece that suits the constitution of that jeep."

On the trip from Mandalay to Bhamo a Columban wrote: "The old traveler keeps behind the baggage wagon and never far from it. Ahead, one may lose touch with it; it may break down and fail to arrive. And it contains all the food and all the bedding. There are no hotels, inns, cafes, or restaurants by the wayside. One knows all that in theory, but one has to learn the hard way what it means in practice. We all did."

There was jubilation in Bhamo when the twelve arrived. The old hands wanted to hear about Cork, Kerry, and Mayo. The morale of the new men improved as they studied maps to locate the Columbans in Bhamo Prefecture, an area 180 miles wide and 342 miles long. Soon they had it memorized.

Jeremiah Kelleher was in Hkudong, caring for 1,200 widely scattered Catholics, parishioners of Father Gilhodes who had died at the close of the war at age seventy-six. High up in Sinlum, Kevin Flatley had a central compound and several schools and chapels in villages. Francis McManamon worked out of Panhkak, near the China border, caring for a widely scattered flock that spoke six languages. The Columban from Melbourne, Bernard Way, and the Chicagoan, Lawrence McMahon, cared for a thousand parishioners and operated six schools in Ting-Sing.

Denis McAlindon was still in Kajihtu where he had operated refugee camps. James Doody had replaced the late Father Thomas Walsh in Namhpalam. Thomas McEvoy was opening mission stations around Sumprabum. Thomas Rillstone had reopened the mission at Jawmaw.

Rebuilding was taking up much time and energy. Daniel Cooney was rebuilding at Meinhkat. James Devine was doing the same at Zaubung. James Cloonan continued to develop Myitkyina. Lawrence Hickey and James McGonagle had reopened Hpunpyen.

The newly arrived Columbans were given assignments for language study. Edward Magee and Gerald O'Brien went to study Shan under direction of Father James Foley at Nanhlaing, ten miles from Bhamo.

In Bhamo, Owen Rodgers, Kieran Collier, Daniel McGeown, James Fitzpatrick, Daniel Treanor, and John O'Sullivan studied Kachin under Father Edmund McGovern.

The remaining four, Joseph O'Hagan, Patrick Madden, James Feighery, and Austin Sands, went to Tanghpre to learn Kachin from Father John Howe.

What lifted the hearts of the young missionaries more than anything was seeing new missions being started. Take Tanghpre, for instance.

Although Father McAlindon had built a school there before the war, it was scarcely more than clumps of debris when Father John Howe arrived in July of 1945.

Within a year he had built a rude presbytery, a chapel, and a boarding school. Three structures of bamboo and thatch, no more substantial than baskets, were all that stood when Fathers O'Hagan, Sands, Madden, and Feighery arrived to study Kachin.

With this mission compound as a center, Father Howe said he hoped to establish a Christian village. The four priests agreed that he could find no lovelier place to realize his dream. Best of all, Father Howe could have as much land as he wanted at this dramatic spot where two rivers coming down from the Himalayas join to form the Irrawaddy.

During a walk around the clearing, the veteran missionary told his confreres that he had experimented in the past year and found the virgin soil excellent for farming, especially since it is enriched periodically by silt from the Irrawaddy. With most of the ground a dense tangle of jungle, it would take a long time to clear unless he could afford to hire plenty of labor. Once cleared he did not want to work the soil the way people in other villages did, little patches cultivated each year; he dreamed of dispensing with bullocks in favor of tractor-drawn ploughs.

The irrigation problem would soon be solved, he said, with pipe that had been used by the military to pump oil along the Ledo Road from India to China. Water from the hills two miles away would come via the line, well-laid and permanent, through a jungle clearing cut wide and kept open. Water would make possible rice fields, a rice mill, and a sawmill.

The sawmill, Father Howe said, was high on his list of dreams. "It is absolutely necessary if we are to avoid the cost of new bamboo buildings every four or five years. Good timber is in easy reach. The Irrawaddy is at our doorstep to transport it. This would be a blessing to the many mission stations—please God—we'll have around us in the near future."

Father Howe explained why Tanghpre, so nicely set in a ring of hills, was an ideal place to develop a mission compound. Many Kachins from the wildernesses of the north cannot help but become aware of it because they use the paths through there and stop at the confluence to rest on their way to Myitkyina. Their backs bent under loads of vegetables, fruit, and sesame seed, they plod down to the bazaar thirty miles south. After trading for salt, rice, thread, and cloth they make the long trek back under equally heavy loads. So it has been for centuries.

Father Howe said that when he told the people of Tanghpre, a village of five houses, about his dream, they were pleased with his enthusiasm and applauded the plan. Then gently, very gently, he revealed their guilty secret—Tanghpre was not healthy, no school should be built there.

In prewar days that would have been the death of the dream, but in 1945 American forces were still in Myitkyina and John Howe knew exactly what an efficient U. S. Army insecticide team could do to the most disease-ridden countryside. With the wholehearted cooperation of his American friends the area was made safe.

Tanghpre was a healthy spot when Father Howe left for a rest in Ireland in 1947. Father Feighery took over the parish, a school with nearly a hundred pupils, a large vegetable garden, and an irrigated rice plantation. The garden produced potatoes, tomatoes, beans, peas, cabbages, and onions, a greater variety than had ever been found in those hills.

Teachers and pupils cultivated the rice plantation and the garden. The plan was that everyone should understand farming; eventually the more academic students would attend high school and the rest would be established on small farms in the area.

Father Feighery began to reap the fruit of Father Howe's foresight and initiative. When small Catholic communities sprang up all over the semicircular tract within a forty-mile radius, the new missionary found himself a much-traveled man. There were distant communities to visit, catechumens to instruct, baptisms to confer, sick to visit, all in widely separated places. Families who had eked out a bare living for centuries planting rice on steep hillsides bordered by jungle saw the benefits of lowland farming and moved down to the plain.

When Father Howe returned from Ireland he was appointed superior of the Columban headquarters in Bhamo and Father Feighery remained as pastor of Tanghpre until assigned to Mogok in central Burma. When Father Francis McManamon became pastor he wrote:

"Today there are forty families in the village, the majority of them Catholic, each of which makes a tidy living cultivating the plain which six years ago was under a mantle of semitropical jungle. The Catholic community that Father Howe envisaged has become a reality; a community where Benediction of the Blessed Sacrament, May Devotions, Stations of the Cross during Lent, and even an annual retreat are part of the people's normal life. In a district where formerly there was not a Catholic, Tanghpre has become the center and inspiration of a parish of 500.

"There are three schools in the parish and this year, 1951, the original school in Tanghpre, with 150 pupils, has become a post-primary school. Many former students attend St. Columban's high school in Myitkyina; those whose education ceases with primary grades are equipped to commence farming. Three teachers and six catechists who not long ago were students in Tanghpre are working in the district."

While Father Howe was developing Tanghpre, Father James Stuart was founding Mogokzup, forty-one miles west of Myitkyina. It was started in 1946 when some of the homeless Kachins he had known in the war said that they wanted to become Catholics.

When Father Stuart suggested that they found a village along the Ledo Road, four families settled at the confluence of two mountain streams and before long there were twenty houses. By the time the young Columbans arrived, Father Stuart was ministering to fifty families in an area that a few years earlier had not heard of the Catholic Church.

Fifty-nine adult Kachins presented themselves for baptism at Christmas. Of the occasion James Stuart wrote: "I baptized all of them at a single ceremony between my second and third Masses on Christmas morning. It took me four hours, but I loved every moment of it because these people are my closest friends. Some were my constant companions during the war. The day of their baptism was really one of the happiest days of my life."

The young priests newly arrived in Burma were delighted with the way Father Stuart could dramatize anything into an amusing story. In describing the baptism he said: "I had to ask them to move forward in groups of two or three at a time. Any movement of the crowd in unison would have caused the bamboo church to collapse. I kept thinking about the time a large group of Kachins gathered in the bamboo shack that I called home. I did some simple coin tricks which delighted them so much they stood and shouted for more. This sudden movement caused my humble abode to collapse. My act had brought down the house!"

After the baptism ceremony Father Stuart organized some sports for the young people. "No world records were broken or even endangered. There were, however, a few startling innovations. For example, the boys jumped from the wrong side of the high jump. The lath was too easily knocked down, they explained, unless the notches on which it rested faced the jumper."

That evening the villagers of Mogokzup and the schoolchildren presented a concert and a nativity play. Because of difficulties it went on until almost dawn of St. Stephen's Day. The delay was caused by a controversy between players and audience over lighting arrangements.

"I had arranged a reflector on a pressure lamp to light up the stage and shield the eyes from the glare. The actors did not like it this way; they altered the position of the reflector to light up the faces of the audience. As a result the players on stage became almost invisible to onlookers. We protested against this change, but the players were resolute. This was the way they wanted it.

"Unless they could see me they did not wish to continue with the performance. I felt flattered, indeed, and was quite prepared to sit and enjoy my popularity, but everyone else objected. Finally the whole affair was settled when someone removed the reflector altogether. The glaring light was then suspended right in front of the stage. This blinded both players and audience, but nobody seemed to mind."

Such old hands as Father Stuart were always trying to get the young missionaries to talk about things back home while they, in turn, kept wanting to hear about the war years. The new men noticed that those who had suffered through the war played down its hardships and tended to tell anecdotes favorable to the Japanese, as though trying to bind up the wounds.

Two of those anecdotes, told by Father Lawrence McMahon, should suffice for examples:

A Japanese soldier entered the church in Bhamo, hastily scribbled a note in French and left it on the altar; "I am a student of the Society of Mary. I have taken charge of your sacred relics and chalice. I will give them to the first priest I meet on the way." He did just that, at Lashio, and eventually the objects were returned to Monsignor Usher.

When a Japanese soldier came to the leper asylum in Mandalay, one of the Columbians dramatized the need for medicine by pantomiming the chills and fever of malaria. The soldier took off on the double and soon returned with a single Atabrine tablet, his daily ration, which he offered with all the goodwill in the world.

The twelve new Columbans, the first to arrive after the war, were getting settled when Monsignor Usher returned from a holiday in Ireland early in 1947. As soon as he reached Bhamo he wrote to a priest back home: "What I was not prepared for was the leap up of the heart when I saw old Burma again. I am still astonished at it, and enormously happy about it."

The trip up to Mandalay, he admitted, was tiring. Travel was by day only because two trains had been derailed and shot up, with heavy loss of life. Revolution had come to Burma. The journey took thirty-six hours instead of the normal fourteen.

"In Mandalay we visited the old remembered places of the bad days. Poor Bishop Faliere is heavily overworked, being bishop, pastor of two parishes one hundred miles apart, procurator, and odd-jobs man all in one."

At Lashio the monsignor stopped to visit Mother Ann Mary, an Italian nun. "I consider her to be one of the bravest little women in all the world. It was my privilege in the bad times to do her two good turns— once when she had been pierced by a couple of machine-gun bullets. These two are my chief hope of being let off lightly at the Judgment."

As he approached Bhamo, groups of Kachins and Shans met him on the road. They had come from miles away in the jungle bearing the traditional gifts of chicken, eggs, fruit, and beer. First a hymn, then handshakes and the presentation of gifts. The monsignor said a few halting words, overcome with the feeling of affection, gave a blessing, and moved on. In Bhamo—Glory be!—he found a new home waiting.

Patrick Usher ended the letter admitting that his bones were tired after so much journeying, but giving assurance that he would not change places with any man, woman, or child in the world. "I tell you it is worth enduring a holiday for the joy of coming back."

Seventeen

HUNGER FOR LEARNING

The Columbans were now thoroughly accepted. As Monsignor Usher explained: "During the war years Fathers McAlindon and Stuart built up a fund of Kachin friendships from which all the priests benefited on their return. Catholic soldiers also had a great influence. Americans and Kachins knelt side by side on Sunday to receive Holy Communion. Those soldiers accomplished by example in a few moments what we had been trying to accomplish for years."

The way Patrick Usher's silver jubilee was celebrated shows the affection the Columbans enjoyed. In March of 1949 several thousand people gathered in Bhamo for three days to honor the monsignor on his twenty-five years as a priest.

"Never before have the Catholics of North Burma come together in such numbers," wrote Father Patrick Madden. "Ninety percent of them have come long distances. Even those who rode the last stages of their journey on lorries have walked for one or two days from their villages to the nearest motor road. Others, from Myitkyina and Tanghpre in the north, have spent twelve hours on the way and have arrived tired and hungry and covered with dust, yet happy that despite burst tires and oiled-up plugs they have at last reached Bhamo.

"A few minutes ago, before I took up my position on the verandah, I had a few words with an aged couple. They have come from Namhpalam, sixty-five miles away, a three-day journey, walking every mile of the way. After the feast they will walk back again."

In a seemingly unending stream, visitors poured into the mission compound by foot, pony, truck, jeep, and bullock cart. The Kachin hill people were in the majority; their gowns mixing red and silver into the crowd and their turbans adding touches of white and yellow. The Shans brought blue to the assembly and the Burmese a blaze of many colors.

From the verandah Father Madden wrote, "I can distinguish Spanish and Shan, Australian and Karen, Italian and Bengali, British and Burmese, New Zealander and Gurkha, Irish and Chinese."

The ceremonies began each morning with a Solemn Mass and the choir gave of its best. At the *sanctus,* at a muffled word of command, officers of the new Burma moved into position before the altar. At the elevation swords flashed and a section of buglers rendered the royal salute.

After breakfast on the first morning, visitors assembled in the open air to pay homage to Monsignor Usher in five languages. The guest of honor received a silver sword and a shoulder bag decorated with silver hangings, gifts given only to a great chief.

When Patrick Usher rose to reply, it was evident that he was deeply touched. After a few honorific generalities, he spoke of the schools that the Columbans had started and of those they would soon be starting. No subject, at that time, was closer to the hearts of the people of upper Burma; nothing the monsignor might say would more enlarge their affections for the Columbans. Ever since the war they had been especially hungry for education, having seen things that they wanted for themselves, or at least for their children.

They had noticed that even the lowliest GI, when on a rest break, might lean against a banyan tree and begin to read. (The military published thirty well-known books each month in editions shaped to fit the pocket of a combat jacket.) They had observed that no sooner did the U.S. Army take a town than it began a daily mimeographed newspaper to keep the soldiers informed. They had noticed that when the sound of gunfire died down the Americans established radio stations; all through the hills the tribesmen listened to "Praise the Lord and Pass the Ammunition" and "Don't Sit Under the Apple Tree with Anyone Else but Me," as the disc jockey said, "Coming to you from beautiful downtown Bhamo!"

Radio was the tribesmen's delight. One day a Columban demonstrated how short-wave can bring broadcasts from India, Japan, Europe, and the United States. All agreed that it was wonderful, until a little old lady well back in the corner said, "Now let's hear what they are saying in Panghkak." The Columban admitted that radio has its limitations. "What good is it," she asked, "if you can't hear what is going on in the next village?"

Yes, the war had impressed the people of upper Burma with the possibilities of technology. They stood in awe of all those jeeps, trucks, bulldozers, and planes. They watched the Ledo Road being cut through dense mountainous jungle at the rate of a mile a day. They saw tons of supplies being flown from India to China. These are the fruits of education, they told each other. Let's have more schools!

Boarding schools are needed, explained the monsignor in his silver jubilee speech, because distances in the hills are so great and paths so uncertain that children cannot be expected to attend as day pupils. Since boarding schools are expensive, he asked that every student pledge in his heart that if he is successful in a career he will in turn help another deserving student.

The Columbans will stress primary schools first, said the monsignor; then will follow middle schools, and finally high schools.

And so the plan unfolded. Within a decade there were forty-seven primary schools, six middle schools and four high schools. Columban fathers and Franciscan Missionaries of Mary conducted two of the high schools in Bhamo Town; Columban sisters and Columban fathers conducted the other two in Myitkyina. Kachins from those high schools were enrolling at Rangoon University within a decade after the monsignor's speech.

Patrick Usher was especially interested in a school for catechists. As early as 1940 he opened the first school in Bhamo. A year after the war he reopened it at Nanklaing. Within two years he moved it to a new building near the Columban headquarters in Bhamo. There Fathers Way and McGovern taught Christian doctrine, apologetics, sacred Scripture, and church history. As part of liturgical studies, the Kachins learned to play the organ and to sing Gregorian chant.

To show in what high regard he held these men, Monsignor Usher wrote: "The catechist usually lives in a village where there is no priest and there he leads the people in their devotions. Most of the time he is traveling from village to village instructing children and catechumens and, on occasion, baptizing the dying. Some villages, scattered among hills rising to 6,000 feet, are several days journey from the central mission and can be visited by a priest only twice a year. The catechist accompanies the priest when he does visit these. His knowledge of the people, language, customs, and mentality are of invaluable help to the missionary."

A Kachin press was something else Monsignor Usher dreamed of developing as part of his program of education. He and Father Way shared the dream while imprisoned in Mandalay. How wonderful it would be, they said, to publish a magazine and to print books.

The two catechisms that Father Way had written while held in confinement were eventually printed in Calcutta, an unsatisfactory arrangement. Neither printers nor proofreaders understood Kachin and so the errors were many.

A decade later Father Way was stationed in Tanghpre, where the Mali and Nmai rivers join to form the Irrawaddy, when he made a plea for a Kachin publication. He dramatized the need by describing his far-flung parish:

"Up the side toward India is Hpungin, where we had a man-eating tiger loose this year. Here are another ten villages.

"Thirty-five villages in a stretch of hill country, seventy miles by forty-two miles! How can you contact the Catholics regularly? Here and there are catechists who keep in touch with six or seven villages, but even they can't be everywhere on Sunday.

"I dream of a newspaper that they can read in their homes and aloud to the others on Sunday. You see, nowadays even in the hills, there is always someone who knows how to read Kachin. The hill schools teach Kachin up to the fourth grade, though from then on it is all Burmese. Anyone who has been to school for a couple of years knows how to read Kachin, so someone in the village can read the message on Sundays.

"Sundays could be dreary for the Kachins. What is in a small hill village? Don't talk about television and suchlike. There is not even one radio, phonograph, newspaper of any sort, theatre, amusement park, novel, picture story book, or anything at all. What a field for a news sheet!"

In September of 1956, Father Way published the first issue of *Jinghpaw Kasa,* The Kachin Messenger. The 250 copies—ten mimeographed pages with a cover showing a cross superimposed on the Burma hills—were printed on paper abandoned by the United States Army a decade earlier.

Two years later Father Way moved the "printery" from a room in his presbytery to a new building of good timber. By then he owned a small hand press that turned out 1,000 copies of the magazine monthly.

In another two years, the circulation was over 2,000 and the clatter of some sophisticated machinery was echoing across the hazy green hills. It was an international assembly of technological implements: a printing press from the States, a generator from England, a stitching machine from Hong Kong, and a paper cutter from Rangoon.

Young Kachins were sent to learn the printer's trade at a press operated by Italian missionaries at Toungoo. They were back in Tanghpre in 1960 when a visiting Columban wrote home: "The House of Way opens every morning at 8 and work continues, with an hour break for lunch, until 5. It runs on a 44-hour working week, Saturday being a half day. It pays union wages. Father Way is very proud of the six men on his staff, 'good keen fellows with a pride in their work,' he describes them. Conditions at the plant are so attractive that 'every young lad in the country is trying to get in.' Already two of its employees have married in the village and settled down."

By now Father Way was printing catechisms, prayerbooks, Bible histories, Gospel stories, and handbooks on childcare, housekeeping, and farming.

John Howe told Bernard Way that he had a highly personal reason for being pleased that books were now printed in Burma. He recalled the time, a decade earlier, when he and Father Dowling had gone to Calcutta for a shipment of books and fire broke out in the cockpit of the plane. When the radio operator rushed for the fire extinguisher, a soldier yelled something about parachutes.

"I grabbed one," said Father Howe, "but it seemed just a maze of straps. I fumbled around hopelessly. Everybody else was so busy that I was overlooked. They rushed to the exit in the tail of the plane. This concentration of weight in the back was inclined to force the nose upwards. Had this happened the plane would have stalled and a crash would have been certain.

"The pilot sensed this and dove downwards. We did not know he had done this purposely. All we knew was that the plane was going down fast. We had a few bad moments."

Father Way knew that his brainchild, *The Kachin Messenger,* was successful when Father Patrick Madden, his successor, told of an incident in the Bhamo police station. After a young Kachin had shot another on a hunting trip, he was brought to the police station where possible manslaughter charges hung over him. The young man asked to see a priest. Father Madden arrived expecting to commiserate with the hapless hunter. Before he could say anything, the Kachin blurted out, "Father, I paid a subscription to *The Kachin Messenger,* and it's not coming!"

In all his plans for schools, seminaries, and publications, Monsignor Usher showed foresight. He sensed that for the Columbans, the years in Burma were numbered. That is why he was in a hurry to develop an educated laity, catechists, and vocations to the religious life.

"The foreigner is being replaced at every level in secular affairs," he wrote as early as 1954. "Why not in the religious sphere also?

"And where there are national religions, the national feeling is against admitting foreigners of another faith, whose conversion work is regarded as setting up divisions within the State. Therefore, in many countries it is becoming increasingly difficult to get entry permits for new missionaries from abroad, and hence arises a new urgency about finding and training local candidates for the priesthood. Anyhow, for many a year, the popes have been urging on all missionaries the formation as soon as possible of a native clergy."

These sentences made Patrick Usher sound less optimistic than usual, and yet they were prophetic. He saw changes coming. There was no turning back to prewar simplicities.

Eighteen

NEEDS OF THE BODY

If there was one thing that Father Timothy Connolly did not expect to find in the jungle it was a slum. And yet, as noted before, when the Superior General of the Columbans visited Burma, he found that compared with the jungle slums, city slums enjoyed a high standard of living.

Slums, of course, breed disease. In speaking of this Dr. Gordon Seagrave, author of *Burma Surgeon,* told Patrick Usher that he could assume that all streams and wells were full of the amoebae that bring dysentery. He added, "If in a strange jungle village you want to know where the village latrine is, just follow the pigs and they will lead you there."

The monsignor was aware that the Malaria Commission, financed by the Rockefeller Foundation, had said that villages of the Chin and Naga hills in Burma have the most deadly malaria found anywhere in the world.

That a missionary must concern himself with such health problems was something the Columbans took for granted. From the beginning, the monsignor instructed the missionaries to open dispensaries as soon as possible, and to pray for the day when they could afford clinics.

The first Columban dispensary was open in 1938 in Nanhlaing on a trial basis but was not especially successful. In those prewar days the people of upper Burma had not yet come to hold Western medicine in high regard. During the war, however, they saw the little miracles worked by medicines with strange-sounding names such as neosalvarsan. Colonel Seagrave said, "Neosalvarsan has as many uses, almost, as bamboo. It will cure syphilis. Intravenously injected and unassisted it will cure a good many malarias and blackwater fevers. It is the best stimulant of the bone marrow ever produced for tropical anemias. Put it into the rectum and it will even cure amoebic dysentery. It brings down the temperature of relapsing fever in twenty-four hours."

After the war, when the dispensary at Nanhlaing reopened, Father James Foley, the pastor, was appalled by the number of Shans who came to him suffering from beriberi. Shans are especially susceptible because they prefer rice so well polished that vitamins have been processed out of it. The nerve disease, the Franciscan Missionaries of Mary told the pastor, causes swelling and disablement of limbs, followed by death.

Father Foley went to Monsignor Usher and expressed his concern about beriberi. When asked what he intended to do about it, the pastor of Nanhlaing said he felt he ought to go to Shingbwiyang, up in the Hukaung Valley, three hundred miles away, and talk with the American doctors.

At Shingbwiyang he found the army disposing of surplus medical supplies, including large containers of vitamin B_1 ampules. The delighted Columban stored the vitamins in his jeep and lurched back across the Ledo Road to Nanhlaing. With pride he presented the cartons to Mother Mary St. Claire, a tall, vivacious French nun who took one look at the ampules and exclaimed, *"Mais oui!"*

Nuns were given injections before the motor had cooled in the jeep. Cures were spectacular with even severe cases responding to Vitamin B_1. The fame of Nanhlaing dispensary was born that day in 1946. The Day of the Golden Needle, the Shans called it.

Soon 25,000 patients were being treated each year. From 8:30 in the morning until noon and from 2:30 until 5:30 they arrived by foot, bicycle, jeep, and bullock cart. Some came by boat along the Taiping and were carried up the river bank in deck chairs.

In many cases a trip to Nanhlaing resembled a family excursion with patients accompanied by relatives and friends bearing food, cooking pots, and bedding. After finding lodging in a hostel in the village, even the healthy ones would ask to be prodded with the golden needle.

Fortunately, by the time the patients had fully accepted Western medicine, the new dispensary was in use. The three-room brick building, thirty-five by twenty-two feet, was inelegant, but to the nuns it was beautiful because they remembered the prewar dispensary—a single room, twelve by five feet, with a cramped verandah.

Most of the patients were Buddhists. At times when Buddhist monks from monasteries in Mandalay, Katha, and Myitkyina were in Bhamo for a festival, they would travel the extra ten miles to be treated at the Nanhlaing dispensary.

Many patients in traveling fifty or more miles would go right past the free government hospital to reach the unpretentious dispensary. Father Foley thought that the great attraction was the personal care and kindly treatment, a specialty of the nuns.

Sometimes it was necessary to send a patient to the hospital, but this was not easy. Kachins have little faith in hospitals. "Too many people die in them," they say.

The "hospital debate" was one that Columbans argued time and time again in tiny dispensaries through the hills of upper Burma. The missionary would begin by admitting, "Yes, some people do die in hospitals. Often it is because they waited too long to get there." Then he would cite examples of people who have returned home cured. After describing hospital facilities and praising the excellent staff, he would assure the patient that a priest would pay a daily visit, a promise that pleased even the Buddhists.

Finally, a relative of the patient might launch into a flowery speech: "As our good Father in his wisdom says, it is indeed true that our sick brother should be taken to the big hospital in Bhamo. But he will have to be carried as far as the motor road. We will be happy to perform this work of mercy, but as the way is long and difficult additional bearers will have to be hired and paid. Then there is the matter of the bus fare to the hospital, and the incidental expenses in the big town. We, alas, are poor and have little money. So, in this emergency we turn to him who is indeed our merciful benefactor and true father."

At this point the missionary would realize that he had won and lost all at the same time. There was nothing for him to do but to reach for his wallet.

At his little dispensary in the jungle, Father Lawrence McMahon, the Chicagoan, endured headaches typical of those suffered by other Columbans. Especially on Sunday mornings.

"As soon as I leave the church I find myself the center of attraction from an eager crowd. A few of the faithful are waiting right outside the sacristy door. Others are gathered at the front door of the church. And there will be another group on the porch of my house. These have not come to congratulate me on my Sunday sermon or to consult with me on a point in canon law. They are here to carry away the drugs that they know are hidden in my medicine cabinet.

"There is an unwritten law here that is strictly enforced: no medicine until the *Jau* has had his breakfast. They accept that, knowing what the *Jau* will be put through after breakfast. They look through the window to make sure I have settled down to eggs and bread before they depart to take rice in preparation for the battle to come."

After breakfast the to-do begins. Kachins talk, and talk fast. They want "sweat medicine" (aspirins), "fever medicine" (antimalarial drugs), "tinsha" (tincture of iodine), "swollen neck" medicine (for goiter).

The missionary listens to a litany of complaints about a racking cough, a persistent headache, sore eyes, aching back. He examines cut fingers, bruised toes, ulcers, and scabies. All the while he keeps trying to reduce the chaos to some semblance of order.

"To cater for a Kachin queue at a dispensary one needs patience, a supply of drugs, patience, and some knowledge of the Kachin language, and patience. There are people everywhere who love to get something for nothing. Someone in the Sunday morning queue will admit to perfect health while asking for 'a complete set,' meaning a sample of every drug in my cabinet. Such people have to be turned away with what tact one can muster."

The Columbans prayed for patience when dealing with those who sneered at certain medicines. For instance, when a new antimalarial drug came out, the Kachins belittled it because it was not bitter. "Whoever heard of a fever remedy that's not bitter!"

A man with mild dysentery refused to accept the white sulfaguanadine tablets that Father McMahon offered him. "No, no, not that! I want the liquid medicine. Father Way cured me with the liquid medicine. That was before the war. I want the liquid medicine!"

Father McMahon's patience was paper thin that day. "I explained as patiently as I could that the drug I was giving him was not aspirin and that if he took it according to directions I'd guarantee a cure. I added, a little sarcastically, that I had no objection to his calling in Father Way; that I would be delighted to hold a consultation with Father Way, but that Father Way was 120 miles distant. My patient agreed, reluctantly, to take the sulfa drug. He was up and around the next day, and I heard no more about the liquid medicine."

What took the most patience was trying to get the Kachins to follow directions. They reasoned: if one tablet brings an improvement, many tablets taken all at once should effect a prompt cure.

"I treated a lad for recurrent malaria before going on to the next village," said Father McMahon. "But before leaving I gave him twelve Atabrine tablets, explaining carefully that he was to take one tablet three times a day for four days. To make sure that he understood, I took the precaution of getting the local teacher to repeat the instructions after me. A few days later I was horrified to hear from the teacher that the boy had taken all of the tablets at once. I explained the danger of Atabrine poisoning and stressed that the lad should be sent down to the hospital in Bhamo if any toxical symptoms appeared. The teacher promised to keep the boy under observation, though I could see that he considered me an alarmist. Subsequently, in answer to further anxious enquiries, I was assured that the boy was well and back in school. He has not had malaria since!"

Anyone operating a dispensary in Burma soon comes to realize that nature in those hills is not benign. Monsoons, insects, snakes, elephants, and tigers, all have a way of disrupting physical well-being.

Father Gerard O'Brien tells a story about a wild elephant who trampled and severely mauled a villager. The man, clearing a field in the hills, sat down to sharpen a *dah,* a swordlike implement. Just then an elephant came up from behind, picked him up with a swoop of trunk and carried him for twenty feet. When distracted by the screams of the man's wife, the beast dropped its victim and stepped on him.

When Father O'Brien arrived he had to shoulder his way through a crowd of neighbors gathered outside the victim's bamboo home. "I found him lying on the floor, covered with a blanket, his terrified wife and family around him. His right leg was roughly bandaged with old rags. Now, I am no doctor, but when I examined the leg what I saw was most alarming and not at all pleasant to look at. All the flesh from the knee to the ankle had been torn away and the bones of his leg laid bare. The foot was twisted grotesquely and some of the bones were missing. His chest, too, had been crushed when the elephant picked him up with its trunk.

"He was in great pain and there was no time to lose in getting him to the hospital in Bhamo, thirty difficult jungle miles away. I stumbled back down the hillside to the road in hopes of finding a passing jeep or truck. I knew that every vehicle in this country is overcrowded, and to find a place for a man with a leg like Labau's was not going to be easy. I put the whole matter in the care of St. Joseph. In a short time a private Land Rover came along, with only four people aboard. Very unusual. The occupants readily consented to take the injured man to Bhamo."

Father O'Brien ran back, panting up the steep hill only to find that Labau's wife was being stubborn about letting him go to a hospital. A neighbor had told her that the doctor might amputate.

In vain Father O'Brien pleaded. He spoke of gangrene but that meant nothing to the wife. Not until night came on and the shock began to wear away and pain increased, did Labau's wife suddenly decide to take him to the hospital. Early the next morning she hired a jeep.

"The following day I saw him in the hospital," said Father O'Brien. "By that time the leg had been straightened, but the doctors were still very doubtful whether it could be saved. I returned a week later and the danger seemed to have passed. The Kachin is a tough and wiry customer and the stuff he is made of is good."

No Kachin is tough or wiry enough to withstand a tiger's attack. Rarely is there an argument about whether or not the victim should go to Bhamo hospital after a tiger strikes. Usually the body is not found.

One Sunday after Mass, Father Way was talking to some excited Kachins in Tanghpre about a man-eating tiger on the prowl. Of five people killed in the past month one had been a parishioner. Now a messenger arrived to say that another parishioner was dead.

The messenger reported that at Mazup Yang, thirty miles away, Mrs. Jingmang, a widow with four children, was returning from clearing her hill field, where she had spent the morning cutting down trees and bamboo, when the tiger struck. At midday she had disappeared from within 300 yards of the village.

When she did not return that evening, the elders guessed the trouble but they did not dare to go out at night. Next morning they sent out trackers who followed the tiger's trail from where it had seized the woman until they found her mangled remains.

Father Way had word, a few days later, that another Catholic, Peter Shamyen La, had been taken fifteen miles from where the widow's body was found. Two pagan animists had also been seized. The people of the territory were beside themselves with fright.

"I decided that I had better go there," said Father Way. "On the second afternoon I arrived at Dinghkru Kawng, where we have a school. As we chatted around the fire that night I heard the tragic details. Mr. and Mrs. Shamyen went out to clear their field in a steep, lonely spot apart from the rest of the villagers. He was felling a tree and when it was about ready he told his wife to move out of the way. She replied that she was quite safe, but he insisted that she move up to higher ground. That was the last she saw of her husband. She heard the growl of a tiger. Her dog dashed down but came running back immediately. Mrs. Shamyen rushed back to the village to give the alarm, but no one would venture out.

"The elders sent to other villages for help. Finally the catechists and teachers and a band of Kachins formed a search party. With a gun and spears they followed the track of the tiger until they found a few bones deep in a ravine."

Father Way decided to go to that spot and offer Mass for the repose of the victim's soul. The village chief insisted that he travel surrounded by a guard. So under a spear escort—spears eight feet long, four in front and four behind—the Columban walked the jungle trail. Cautiously the party went through rocky ravines, with everyone peering warily into the deep, dark tangle.

At Woihtup Uga village where Shamyen La came from, the Catholics were wild with joy when Father Way arrived. They had felt deserted in their trouble because other villagers were too frightened to visit them. The missionary had with him a stereoscopic viewmaster with reels of the canonization of Pius X, the Passion Play, and views of Chicago and New York. He thought that the pictures might help take the villagers' minds off their troubles.

In the Chicago scenes an eight-lane highway appeared, causing much comment in the audience. Father Way turned to the elders and said, "Do you know that more people might be killed in one week on such highways than a tiger would kill in years up here? Yet people are not afraid to go out in a car."

"That is quite right," agreed the catechist. "When we go to Myitkyina we take a jeep from Tanghpre and have no fear, though there might be an accident. But with the tiger, we feel he can be anywhere. It's a terrible feeling that a big, silent cat may be waiting to give you a horrible death."

To add to the health problems, nature has given Burma three seasons: the cold from October to February, the hot from March to June, and the rainy from June to October, and each brings its own favorite illnesses. As season gave way to season the dispensaries grew in popularity. The clinic that Patrick Usher hoped for was not built until nearly two decades after the war, however. It was established only then because of the arrival of some special people. More of that later.

Nineteen

A GOOD MAN DIES

The spring before his death Monsignor Usher wrote with enthusiasm about the dedication of the new church in Myitkyina. The zest of the celebration brought back memories of his own silver jubilee, and the presence of Archbishop Faliere recalled the early days in Burma. The celebration itself, and the summing up that it engendered, brought satisfaction to the ailing priest, who at fifty-nine was beginning to look older.

The committee for the church dedication, organized by Fathers Howe and Dowling, planned to house 5,000 visitors. Temporary structures of bamboo and thatch were erected in the mission compound; fireplaces were built and piles of wood stacked.

In describing how 9,000 guests were fed at one meal, the monsignor wrote: "I do not have the menu to send you, but here are some totals to suggest what a feast it was: 340 baskets of rice, 23 cows, 13 buffalo, 4 hogs, plus potatoes and pumpkins beyond measure."

On Monday the weekly plane from Rangoon and Mandalay brought all of the bishops of Burma to Myitkyina. They had decided to hold their annual meeting there so as to be on hand for the dedication. The new rectory, just completed, was ready to receive them. Their own affairs kept them occupied until Friday.

As visitors streamed in from the jungle all day Friday, they were met at the gate and escorted to their places as drums beat, cymbals clashed, and banners waved. Here and there a flute and a mouth organ added to the dissonance. And yet as darkness fell, quiet settled over the encampment. A dozen priests were busy in the confessionals until nine o'clock when several thousand voices recited the rosary.

Saturday was Dedication Day. Although the ceremony did not start until 7:30, most visitors attended Mass at six o'clock in a temporary meeting hall. They knew that distribution of the sacrament would be

impossible among the tightly packed congregation at the main ceremony.

Eight bishops and twenty priests walked in the procession that accompanied Archbishop Faliere to the blessing of the church. The pastor, Father Howe, sang the High Mass. The auxiliary of Mandalay,
Bishop Joseph U Win, preached the sermon in Burmese.

The presence of Albert Faliere and Joseph U Win brought the monsignor memories of the afternoon twenty-two years earlier when the
two of them had greeted him on the railroad platform in Mandalay.
Bishop U Win recalled that day too, observing that at the time, 1936,
the Catholic community of upper Burma had numbered only 3,500.
Thanks to the Columbans the number had increased to 20,000. Nineteen churches and sixty-eight mission stations; eighteen clinics and
eighteen orphanages now stood in an area that had but four churches
twenty-two years ago. A chain of sixty-one elementary schools, two
junior high schools, and four high schools link together the widely
scattered missions.

Patrick Usher looked around trying to estimate the size of the congregation. "Nobody succeeded in counting the people inside the
church; it was the maximum number of small, light people that could
be squeezed into 4,500 square feet of floor space from which all furniture had been removed. The others made the best use they could of
doors and windows."

In his Dickensian style, the monsignor described the procession of
the Blessed Sacrament that moved along the public roads on Saturday
afternoon. "It was a most impressive spectacle in the place and circumstances, with the long lines moving in excellent order, the de-
meanor reverent, hymns and prayers in unison, banners and bright
colors everywhere. Processions are beloved of all classes here. The ordinary ones feature ingeniously decorated trucks, the maximum of
noise from drums and horns, and the participants trailing along in
good-humored disorder. They find ours different and they like the dignity and reverence of them."

Four hundred children and adults received the sacrament of confirmation on Sunday. Archbishop Bazin of Rangoon sang the Pontifical
High Mass and Bishop George U Kyaw preached in Burmese.

The final event was the procession of Our Lady as the sun went
down on Sunday. In the stillness of a perfect evening, lighted candles
encircled the sixteen-acre mission grounds. Old, well-loved hymns

were sung with enthusiasm, and decades of the rosary filled the spaces between.

"The particular joy of the Myitkyina feast was that nearly all the participants were new to the Church," wrote Patrick Usher in comparing the past with the present. "Twelve years ago, the present mission grounds were still open fields with no trace of or thought of the convent, girls' high school, boys' high school with its boarding section, the rectory, and the church of today. The whole district could boast of only 395 Catholics then."

While comparing the past with the present, the monsignor must have considered the changes in his health, something that would have to be listed on the minus side of the ledger. He was not one to speak of it, and if someone asked how he felt, he had a way of turning the conversation back upon the questioner. Patrick Usher was not an ideal patient. For instance, when a doctor gave him vitamin pills they ended up in the hands of his barber. A Columban said, "By nature he was always reticent about taking extra rest and observing the precautions the state of his health demanded." Another added, "You know what a horror of hospitals he had. The very mention of taking treatment at home even was enough to arouse all the power of his stubbornness."

He was "not in good form," as the Irish say, throughout the summer of 1958. He suffered pains in his left shoulder and arm, the side that would eventually become paralyzed.

As secretary to the conference of bishops in Rangoon, in August, he worked hard and had only one hour's sleep a night. The strain caught up with him, though. While distributing communion his left hand went lame; he kept the ciborium from falling by pressing it against his chest.

Father Fisher and Mother Kevin, the Good Shepherd provincial, appealed to him to have a medical checkup, but he waved them off and left for Bhamo. There he biked, three times in two weeks, to Nanhlaing ten miles away, to get injections. His left hand and leg continued growing numb and powerless.

Father Cloonan called Dr. Tan Kyi Lin, who was shocked when he saw the monsignor. How he had aged! The doctor suspected incipient paralysis but before making a final judgment called in the civil surgeon. His diagnosis: a case of collapse of nerves due to vitamin deficiency. Vitamin treatment, the surgeon said, would restore the appetite within two weeks, and it did.

The hand and leg showed no improvement, however, and soon there was a noticeable droop developing on the left side of the mouth. At this point Father Cloonan sent to Myitkyina for Father Howe.

"When I arrived on Tuesday, October 7, the monsignor looked pretty well," wrote Father Howe. "I told him he would have to go home for treatment, not necessarily to Dublin, but at least to London, and that Father Paddy Conneally could go with him. He didn't turn down the idea point blank, and I took that as his way of submitting to it, knowing him as I did.

"Next morning, however, he told me he had had a very bad night. He kept himself awake for hours thinking over the proposal I had made about going home and marshalling all the possible arguments against it. When I heard that, I decided that for the present anyway, the only place for him was here, so I assured him that we would not send him home until he was well. He got into great form then, talking and joking about old times."

Two months earlier Patrick Usher had written to a friend: "For a year or two back I have been talking about 1959 as the year I would go home. Now it is fixed. I have asked for a leave of absence from March 15 to October 15, that is to say for all the year that is worth having."

He wanted to return to County Louth, where he had been born at Tullyallen, May 12, 1899, and see once more Ireland's hawthorne hedgerows in May. Of course he would have to be back in Burma in time to be consecrated as the first bishop of the Diocese of Bhamo. The ceremony was to be held at Christmas in 1959 in the new Saint Patrick's, a cathedral that was being built even as he lay dying. He had set the date, October 26, the Feast of Christ the King, for the blessing of the cornerstone, but he would not live to see that ceremony.

Thursday afternoon, the day that Pope Pius XII died, Fathers Howe and Magee found the monsignor collapsed on the floor of his room unable to move. As they put him to bed they noticed that his speech was much thicker. When the doctor arrived, he still insisted that it was not a stroke, but that the nerves were upset as the result of shock caused by the fall.

On Friday the patient had still greater difficulty in speaking. Late that evening Father Howe anointed him and called in a nurse for the night. On Saturday morning Dr. Tan again brought the civil surgeon, who at first glance said that the monsignor had suffered a stroke and should be taken by ambulance to the hospital immediately.

"By midday, Sunday, he was weaker, so at four o'clock I gave him the last blessing and recited the prayers for the dying," said Father Howe. "He was still quite conscious at that time and made a brave effort to make the sign of the cross. From then on there were several priests and sisters with him until his death at 3:45 on the morning of Monday, October 13, 1958.

"He had a grand death but a fighting one, coming back several times, like the pope, for a few more breathers. And almost with his last gasp he stuck out his chin in a typical gesture."

Chinese carpenters made the coffin with care. Masons working on the new cathedral paused to line the grave with brick and cover it with concrete.

Twenty-one priests arrived in time for the funeral. They recited the Solemn Office at seven o'clock Tuesday morning and afterward Father Howe sang the Requiem High Mass.

Beneath a scorching sun, thousands of mourners walked the two miles to the Bhamo Christian cemetery, reciting the rosary in many languages along the way. They found that Patrick Usher's grave was near those of Fathers Walsh and McGeown and not far from a few French priests who had known the Kachin hills.

Members of many creeds stood at the graveside. Baptist schools had closed their doors so that students and teachers might attend the funeral. A Buddhist commissioner said: "He is very dear to me as he is to all, particularly the residents of Bhamo. He once expressed the desire to become a Burmese national. That desire is partly fulfilled in that he died in Burma and was buried in Burmese soil. He really loved Burma and his services to our country will always be remembered with profound gratitude. His untimely death will be mourned by many, irrespective of race or religion. In him I have lost a friend and a golfer."

At the time, Father Howe recalled that a fatherly thoughtfulness was Patrick Usher's outstanding characteristic: "He encouraged rather than drove his priests. He never missed an opportunity to show that he had confidence in them, and whenever we came to headquarters for business or on the annual retreat, the example of his life, unassuming, humble, dedicated, did more to inspire us than the most thoroughly compiled manual of discipline and rules could ever have done."

Father Foley added, "Certainly he did not appear before God with empty hands."

Twenty

NEW CATHEDRAL, NEW BISHOP

Although Sunday, October 26, came but ten days after the funeral, Father John Howe, the vicar-general, decided that the foundation stone for the new church should be blessed on that date. He was aware that the monsignor, as his last official act, had selected the day, giving as his reasons that it was the Feast of Christ the King and that it came in the middle of the annual priests' retreat, the only time of year all Columbans gathered in Bhamo.

Kachins, Burmans, Shans, and Tamils crowded into the old bamboo and mud plaster church for the Mass that preceded the blessing of the stone. The visiting priests had to wait outside, making evident the need for a larger structure. Among them were the two newest Columbans, Fathers David Wall and Colum Murphy, who had been in Burma scarcely a week.

Father Thomas Dowling preached in Burmese and Father Howe in Kachin. Each spoke of Patrick Usher and described the church he had planned.

Looking to the left through the window, the parishioners could see what would eventually be the walls of a cathedral. They were of brick, a suitable material for that climate, and were by now of sufficient height to give some idea of the shape of the final structure. In the middle of the scaffolding loomed a gaunt, wooden cross planted on the spot where the high altar would eventually stand.

The parishioners were told that the building would follow the traditional cruciform design, with a high central nave separated from the low-roofed side aisles by concrete columns. Three rose windows would decorate the church: one over the main door and one in each arm of the transept.

At the end of the Mass, Father Howe went to the wall at the left of the main door where a square niche was ready for the foundation stone. After explaining that according to tradition an opening is left in the cornerstone to hold symbolic objects, he approached it, and placed inside a list of the priests and parishioners who were present, some coins of the Union of Burma, copies of Burmese newspapers containing Prime Minister U Nu's panegyric on the late Pius XII, and reports of Monsignor Usher's death.

Father Howe accepted the silver trowel, presented according to tradition by the contractor. This one had been engraved in advance, for as he used it he noticed the inscription: Presented to Monsignor Usher by Dr. Tan Gyi Lin, Contractor.

After the ceremony the priests and the parishioners walked among the rising walls talking about what a wonderful thing the new church would be. An old Kachin asked Father McMahon how many Catholic churches there are in his native Chicago.

"Three hundred."

"Did you say three?"

"Three hundred."

The old man looked reproachful. He said nothing, but disbelief was all over his face.

By the time the church was ready to be dedicated, John Howe was a monsignor serving in the capacity of prefect apostolic of Bhamo. He set the ceremony for March 14, 1961, observing that the year was an appropriate one for dedicating a cathedral to Saint Patrick since it was the 1500th centenary of the saint's death.

Fifteen thousand Catholics, Hindus, Mohammedans, and Buddhists attended the festivities which began on Tuesday and continued until Thursday. Although the occasion was in the main religious, there was a feast that used 450 bushels of rice, a gift from U Nu, the prime minister of the Union of Burma.

An Australian, Archbishop James Knox, the apostolic delegate, sang the Pontifical High Mass, and another Australian, Father Bernard Way, delivered the sermon. The archbishops of Rangoon and Mandalay, and the prefect apostolic of Akyab attended the ceremony along with the head of the Kachin state and two representatives sent by the prime minister.

The climax of the festivities was a torchlight procession described by one Columban as "a sight reminiscent of Lourdes." During it the Kachins sang the *Credo* in Latin and the *Te Deum* in Kachin.

The Columbans had an added reason for singing the hymn of praise that night. For some time, the rumor had been abroad that they may no longer be welcome in Burma, considering the government's policy of making Buddhism the state religion. At the dedication, however, a message came from the prime minister that put their minds at ease.

U Nu's advisor, U Ohn, read to the assembly in Bhamo a letter addressed to the apostolic delegate:

"I trust Your Excellency will find it possible to announce to the Catholics of Burma my most solemn pledge that there never shall be any discrimination whatsoever on the grounds of race or religion and that, on the contrary, I hope and pray that those who are members of the Catholic Church will flourish and progress, and the church in Burma with them, because I am firmly convinced that the teaching of the church through the bishops and priests accords with that which is highest and noblest in man."

A Rangoon newspaper, *The Nation,* published on its front page, on March 18, the headline: 15,000 KACHINS APPLAUD PREMIER'S ASSURANCE ON RELIGIOUS FREEDOM.

Within a month of the dedication of Saint Patrick's, word reached Burma that Pope John XXIII was raising the prefecture of Bhamo to a diocese and that it would be in charge of the ecclesiastical district of 30,000 square miles of upper Burma, stretching from near Mandalay to Tibet.

When Monsignor Howe became a bishop on July 1, 1961, the ceremony took place in Saint Patrick's, at Bhamo. The archbishop of Rangoon was present, along with two Columban bishops, Harold Henry, from Korea, and Patrick Cronin, from Mindanao. The consecrating prelate was Joseph U Win, archbishop of Mandalay, assisted by George U Kyaw, bishop of Bassein, and Sebastian Shwe Yauk, bishop of Toungoo.

Bishop Howe said how pleased he was that his three consecrators were the first members of the Burma hierarchy to come from the ranks of the local clergy. He observed that the elevation of a prefecture to the full status of diocese usually marks the coming of age of an ecclesiastical district, and this means that the Columbans are well on the road to doing what missionaries everywhere are meant to do, establish a local clergy.

"When the stage is reached, as please God it will in time, that there are sufficient Kachin and Shan priests to take care of the spiritual needs of their own people, the missionary aim of the Society of St. Columban's in Burma will have been happily accomplished."

Twenty-One

ON THE TRAIL

The thirty Columbans were so widely scattered that to visit them Bishop Howe faced formidable travel. Many missionaries could be reached by jeep, but some were hidden in hills so remote that they needed to be searched out by foot or pony.

It was easy enough to reach Father Thomas Rillstone, even though he was 6,000 feet up in the Kachin hills, because an all-weather road covered the twenty-eight miles between Bhamo and his parish in Sinlum. To continue by jeep the thirty miles from Sinlum to Panghkak was another matter. It was impossible during the monsoon and only somewhat possible from November to May, the dry season.

"Even then you will be well advised not to motor it unless you have strong nerves and a sound heart," wrote Father McMahon, who knew that country all too well. "If you do attempt it, you will arrive at Panghkak a little shaken, both mentally and physically. However, you will meet a sympathetic host in Father James Fitzpatrick, the pastor, who has been over that road many times, and knows its terrors."

Since Panghkak village was only five miles from the Chinese border no one could visit there without having the Red Chinese armies in mind. The Red Chinese armies crossed the border from time to time to make the point that China had been unfairly treated in a boundary settlement made with the British many years ago.

This nearness of the Bamboo Curtain worried Father Fitzpatrick only once. When his two ponies, his only means of transport, were stolen in the night and led away in the general direction of China, he felt some concern.

When Father Fitzpatrick died in 1969, Father McMahon wrote: "During his last years in Panghkak he struggled with a major disability which in normal times would have made retirement mandatory. But knowing that the political situation prohibited any replacement he died among his people. The good shepherd."

After the Sinlum-Panghkak jeep run, the bishop was relieved to know that the 25-mile trip to Ting Sing must be made on foot or by pony. Father McMahon had told him: "If you are for an early start, you can complete the trek in one long day. Or if that seems too much for you, you may spend the night with Catholic people in one of the many Kachin villages along the way. A mile outside Ting Sing one of the boys will herald your arrival by a long and melodious blast on a bugle, answered from the village by the pealing of three church bells. That is our way of telling you how glad we are you have come, and how welcome you'll be to stay."

The bishop's visit to Ting Sing to confer the sacrament of confirmation is worth describing in some detail because it is typical of many such trips that he made and that Monsignor Usher had made before him.

The confirmation ceremony among Kachins ranks in importance just behind Christmas and Easter. And it has one thing that lends a glamour lacking even on the great feasts: the presence of the bishop himself, complete with ring, crosier, mitre, and purple. So gongs throb, bells peal, drums roll, and the shout goes out: *Saradaw du na ra ai,* "The bishop is coming!"

Because of the vastness of his diocese—30,000 square miles with one missionary to every 1,000 square miles—the bishop arranged his travel plans at least three months in advance. The pastors also needed to know the date of the ceremony in plenty of time because their parishes were so far-flung.

In Father McMahon's, for example, there were thirty-five villages with houses miles apart even within the limits of one village. After getting out the word to 1,200 Catholics scattered through the hills, the pastor began Operation Cleanup around the compound, church, and presbytery. Since the regular house staff was insufficient in manpower, extra workers from the village volunteered for emergency duty.

The operation took several days and was still in progress when somebody suddenly shouted: "There goes the bugle! Here comes the bishop!" Everybody stopped to listen. There was silence for a moment. Then the faint bugle call in the distance announced that the guests had reached the outskirts of the village and would arrive within the quarter hour.

"There was a headlong rush to the bell tower," said Father McMahon, "and in another moment three bells were rocking and pealing in a joyous salute of welcome. In the out-kitchen the head cook blew up the fire and kept a watchful eye on the water boiling for the bishop's tea and the bishop's bath.

"There were also several youngsters in the kitchen, with no legal status whatever, who kept a wary eye on the door. They knew that they were out of bounds and were prepared to make a hasty exit should the big *Jau*—that's me—see them. However, the *Jau* was not worried for the moment about small boys in the kitchen. He was engaged in a final 'count down' in the bishop's room: Soap? Towels? Bed made properly? Extra blankets? Mr. Conrad Hilton wouldn't be impressed, but he's not a missionary bishop."

Father McMahon hurriedly put on a clean white soutane—two buttons missing, but never mind! By the time he reached the entrance to the compound his parishioners had gathered, listening to the blasts from the bugle increasing in volume and directing all attention to the turn in the trail where the guests would come into view.

"There he is! The bishop!"

"He doesn't look very old."

"Two priests with him."

"Father Devine."

"Father Conneally."

"Shh! Keep quiet now."

Father McMahon welcomed the bishop and knelt to kiss his ring. The crowd closed in and the priests began the kind of banter that men are given to when they have not seen each other for a long time.

"Hi, Larry. You're looking good, but a bit balder, I see!"

"At least I'm keeping my weight down!"

After visiting the church, Bishop Howe and the priests returned to the presbytery for tea and rest. Later, following the evening rosary, Fathers Devine and Conneally heard confessions.

By dawn people from many villages were streaming in dressed in their best and looking fresh despite a walk of from two to ten miles up the hills and down the valleys. Families moved along the narrow paths in single file, a custom that persists even on the widest road. Centuries of walking one behind another has made the habit too strong to overcome. The Columbans were amused to see hill people proceeding in this fashion along the Burma Road, but the tribesmen were probably just as amused to see Columbans trying to walk two and three abreast on a jungle trail with those on the outside taking a pounding from trees and bushes.

In each group the mother carried a large basket on her back, a strap around her forehead supporting the burden. In the basket were the family supplies of rice and other food. Usually the second youngest child sat atop the basket, little legs dangling over the mother's shoulders, and keeping this lofty perch by a firm grip on her head. An older child carried the baby in a wide piece of cloth tied around the shoulders.

"The women usually walk in the lead," observed a Columban. "I don't know why, but there is probably a good reason. I'm sure it is not because of the danger of land mines and booby traps, as some cynics suggested during the war."

Masses were celebrated shortly after dawn and by 8:30 the priests were back at the church. Fathers Devine and Conneally returned to the confessional, and Father McMahon took up a position near the front door of the church, with the parish census book in one hand and a packet of tickets in the other. Each ticket carried a name, village of residence, baptismal registration number, and confirmation name.

"With the distribution of tickets went the usual stern warning that they be not lost," said Father McMahon. "Mothers with babies on their backs were urged to be especially vigilant, since the paper was pink the infants seemed inclined to chew on it.

"I carried the census book for good reason. As always there are some who complain about not receiving a ticket. It had to be proven to them that they had been confirmed in infancy, or while unconscious in grave illness. It was sometimes difficult to convince old people, especially those of the gentle sex. I suspect that those pious ladies were unwilling to accept the decision of the Council of Trent decreeing that the sacrament of confirmation could be received validly but once. I made no mention of Trent, but did show them what the census book indicated. There were times, though, when the book showed that the petitioner was right and I was wrong. So I hurriedly filled out a ticket, apologizing with profusion."

When, after three hours, the last of 250 penitents had been absolved, ringing bells brought 500 worshipers crowding into the church where pews had been removed to make more room. With suitable decorum the ceremony proceeded even when a ticketless diehard attempted to approach the altar rail and had to be turned away ever so gently. After confirmation was administered to 150, the bishop celebrated a high mass at which there were 300 communicants.

"By now, 1:30, it was high time for rice," recalled Father McMahon. "A favored few, such as ex-houseboys and revered elders, sought a handout in the priest's kitchen. Most gathered in family groups to squat in circles on the ground eating curry and rice cooked early that morning at home. After the rice, people gathered to confer the traditional Kachin greeting of honor on the bishop and priests seated in state on the river bank."

After a song of welcome a teacher read a special address written in Kachin rhymed couplets, and with a profound bow presented the ornate manuscript to the bishop. Five young girls came forward dressed in splendid Kachin costumes: red woven skirts with black velvet jackets encrusted with silver ornamentation. They carried baskets containing traditional Kachin gifts: cooked rice, delicacies, fresh eggs, beer, and liquor.

The bishop tasted the beer and liquor, pronounced them excellent, and had them distributed among the elders.

"Beer, made from rice, is not bad when properly brewed," according to Father McMahon. "The distilled liquor is extremely potent and a foreigner is advised to take it with caution. During the war, the U.S. Army suspected the liquor would be detrimental to health. A bottle was flown to a Washington laboratory for analysis and the concluding sentence of the report read: 'This liquid is definitely nonpotable.' "

Among the gifts was the grand gesture, a white soutane enlivened with red buttons and piping, a sensational departure from custom. At committee meetings held to discuss this question many elders had been in favor of the traditional gift of a woven shoulder bag, or a ceremonial sword with silver scabbard.

"I knew that the bishop's room in Bhamo was already overstocked with bags and swords. So I tactfully suggested that a soutane would be more useful and a more acceptable gift. The idea proved too novel for immediate approval, but when I explained that what I had in mind was no ordinary soutane like my own, but a *bishop's* soutane, with buttons and piping in red, the elders agreed with enthusiasm."

After the bishop had given a fatherly address and all had knelt for his blessing, the parishioners approached for an individual introduction. With that the day ended, and the tribesmen set off toward their homes with the wish, "*Ya hpang de bai hkrum* (Let us meet again!)"

From Ting Sing the bishop could travel by pony the 15 miles to

Zaubung with its good church and large, well-kept compound. This was a good place to rest since Father Devine had a comfortable house and a quiet way that was easy to be around. Rest was impossible, though, if the hill people planned a feast, as well they might with the bishop in the neighborhood.

After a full program of religious ceremonies, a feast in the Kachin hills called for an interminable meeting at which catechists, teachers, and wise old men lecture the people for hours on end. The bishop is expected to sit through it and even contribute to the exhortations. Subjects range from the fall of Adam and Eve to the need to get students to school on time. Hymns are sung between speeches.

At a gathering of so many people something exciting is sure to happen. On one occasion when Father Devine was nodding through speeches, a Kachin shook him and excitedly whispered, "Sick call."

"It was a sick call and at the same time it was not," said Father Devine. "There were two patients, both pagan, who needed me chiefly for medical purposes. The two men had met with an accident while trying to kill a buffalo for the feast. The animal, not being tied securely, broke loose and when cornered in the jungle charged and injured the two quite severely."

The work of butchering at the feasts is usually left to the pagans who find it a full-time job. If the Catholics took care of it, a dozen men would find themselves too busy to take part in the spiritual exercises and miss the whole point of the gathering.

"I have tried buffalo meat several times," said Father Devine, "and although I had most of my own teeth I never did succeed in reducing the morsel to a stage where I could swallow it. Someone described the buffalo as the ugliest creature in the animal world and he might have added, the toughest. The meat has the consistency of high-grade leather. Kachins relish it. They have the ability to crack bones with their teeth."

From Zaubung it was necessary to double back three miles to Kaithtik on the Ledo Road, renamed the Union Road. There it was possible to get transport to Bhamo, a thirty-eight-mile trip that could usually be made in two hours but could take as long as eight because of landslides during the monsoon.

Two parishes easy to reach were Namlimpa and Momauk. The sixty-mile trip from Bhamo to Namlimpa could be a pleasant one, especially if the pastor, Father Thomas MacEvoy, drove his Land Rover and helped pass the time with his stories accumulated during twenty years in Burma. He spoke with pleasure of the church he was building, but he did not live to say Mass in it because on Christmas Eve of 1959 he collapsed on the trail and died within minutes.

By the time the bishop began visiting Momauk, ten miles from Bhamo, Father Francis McManamon was pastor of a fine church that had been built by Father Denis McAlindon.

The trip to Hkudung, twenty-eight-miles over motor road, was more daring than it sounds. For the last six miles the bishop's jeep labored up and up along what was little more than a narrow trail. As a Columban said, "If you enjoy thrills, this is the trip for you. If you don't, shut your eyes, pray, and trust your driver."

Just as Patrick Usher had his spirits lifted in 1936 by a visit to Father Gilhodes in Hkudung, Bishop Howe enjoyed a similar lift each time he went there. Father Jeremiah Kelleher and his assistant, Father Michael Healy, were kept more than occupied ministering to the most populous parish in the Kachin hills, with its nine out-churches, all of good solid timber.

They also supervised a large boarding school with nearly 300 students, many of them the grandchildren and great-grandchildren of those Father Gilhodes had tempted with bonbons 60 years earlier; the children who had taught him Kachin while he taught them French.

Sight of the Hkudung church brought to mind the great black buffalo that had stomped around in a pit of yellow mud, churning marle until it could be shaped into bricks. Seeing the great pillars in the church, the bishop recalled the time they lay four miles away, at the bottom of the hill. A decade earlier, Father Bernard Smyth had written: "Six men at least would be needed to carry one of them, although, indeed, I cannot imagine how six men could carry such a weight such a length."

Word got around that Jau Kelleher had a job to be done and two or three groups of those who do such jobs had called on him to make arrangements. On each occasion everything had been settled amicably; terms were agreed upon and a date fixed to begin. Months passed and Father Kelleher heard no more about it, and the pillars remained four miles down the hill.

"If the Lord wants a new church," said the pastor, "He had better soon start showing some interest in it."

Eventually, the Third Kachin Rifles heard of the difficulty and sent twenty of its best infantrymen to help move the heavy posts up a practically vertical mountain path.

Wherever the eye fell a story came to mind. The sight of a diesel generator there in remote Hkudung caused the bishop to recall an anecdote that Father Michael Healy often repeated.

The young priest was scarcely twenty-four hours in Bhamo in 1958 when Monsignor Usher said, "I'm sending you to Hkudung to learn Kachin. Father Jerry Kelleher will teach you. Do you know anything about diesel engines?"

Father Healy said no, but that did not change the appointment in any way.

"I arrived in Hkudung as the angelus bells were ringing," said Father Healy. "I had only to look at Father Kelleher's face to see how welcome I was. But we were scarcely seated when his genial smile faded and he eyed me anxiously. 'Do you know anything about diesel engines?' "

In due course the new missionary was to meet the sisters in their convent, the teachers, and the catechists, but first of all he had to be introduced to a brilliant green diesel generator. The young man followed Father Kelleher as he led the way. Kachins waiting to interview their pastor and patients who had come for treatment at the dispensary joined in the procession.

Father Healy said he felt the eyes of Hkudung were upon him and so he tried to assume an intelligent appraising look. Not knowing what to say he commented on the color, congratulating Father Kelleher on how well the diesel blended into the jungle background.

Father Kelleher as in no mood for levity; that engine had been trouble from the day he heard of it. He recalled that when the news broke in Hkudung that an electric generator was due to arrive excitement ran high and a crowd gathered. As the old jeep pulling its trailer of precious cargo successfully negotiated the final hill a cheer went up.

Then, to the horror of everybody, the jeep, trailer, and generator suddenly plunged down a ravine. The driver jumped clear and was uninjured, but the generator took punishment. Fuse boxes were smashed, wires were disconnected, and the exhaust pipe burst. The main works were intact, though, and by a magnificent feat of engineering with ropes and poles the villagers lifted the generator and trailer back to the trail.

Father Healy finally got the engine going. He never understood how he did it; a miracle, he said.

There were evenings, of course, when lights faded at study time to the delight of boarding students. If the lights went out during Sunday devotions Father Healy would say how wise the church is in her insistence on candles. It wasn't always easy to locate the cause of the breakdown. The young priest's knuckles often ached when an ill-fitting wrench suddenly released its grip on a nut that obstinately resisted.

"There were times," said Father Healy, "that I frankly wished the whole outfit at the bottom of the ravine. And yet if I were asked what was the most useful piece of equipment in a mission station like Hkudung I'd reply, 'A good electric lighting set.' "

The old secondhand equipment gave good service for a few years and then quit completely. After a major breakdown at the plant, Father Kelleher was told that it was impossible to locate new parts for such an old model. He had to resign himself to the fact that not even an "expert" like Father Healy could do anything about it this time.

So much for Bhamo District. From Bhamo Town to Myitkyina the bishop often took a forty-minute flight that seemed longer during the monsoon season. To go by road was slower, of course, but more interesting.

The twenty-eight miles of road from Bhamo to Mainghat was a pleasant enough ride. The pastor of this Shan village, Father Daniel Cooney, was also the superior of the Columbans in Burma.

After twenty more miles along the road, the bishop came to Baw-i village. Father Owen Rodgers lived there and took care of a parish sixty miles long. The fine brick church was built by a former pastor, Father Kieran Collier, in memory of his brother, Father Anthony, who had been killed in Korea in 1950 by soldiers of the Red army.

From Baw-i a two-hour drive over fifty miles of road took Bishop Howe to Kachaw, where he had to cross the Irrawaddy by ferry. Since the boat was small and slow and there was always a line of vehicles waiting, the bishop found plenty of time to read his breviary. From the crossing all the way to Myitkyina the road was good, as roads go in upper Burma. Now he was traveling the district in which the Columbans had made the most progress since the end of the Second World War.

At Myitkyina it was a pleasure to arrive at a splendid and spacious compound. There was plenty of room to spare even though the compound held a large church, separate houses for priests and brothers, primary and secondary schools for boys and girls, boarding dormitories, and a convent for the Columban Sisters. The place was abuzz with activity under the direction of Father Thomas Dowling, the vicar general, and his assistant, Father Eamon Magee.

The excellence of the Myitkyina schools gave the bishop satisfaction. St. Columban's school for boys, elementary and secondary, was conducted by the De La Salle Brothers with Brother Urban as director. Across the compound girls were educated from kindergarten through high school under direction of the Columban Sisters, with Mother Mary Ita as the superior. Both schools employed large staffs of lay teachers.

Twenty-seven miles north of Myitkyina was Tanghpre, a place of special interest to Bishop Howe. As a young priest he had started a village there at the scenic spot where two rivers meet to form the Irrawaddy.

The bishop knew that the printing press at Tanghpre got its power from a diesel generator, but he wondered where the three priests stationed there got *their* energy. Fathers Bernard Way and Patrick Madden conducted a school for catechists and published a magazine, books, and pamphlets. Father James McGonagle was a traveling pastor.

Tanghpre mission covers a vast area including a mountainous district called Hpungyin Dung, parts of which are so steep that the Kachins describe them as *ma hkrap kadawng,* "steep climbs which make the children cry." The territory is so extensive that it took Father McGonagle twelve to fourteen days to walk through it.

To visit more hill parishes the bishop proceeded north on a road, by no means a "freeway," but good enough to allow the jeep to move at ten miles an hour. Upon reaching mile 103 from Myitkyina the bishop would get out and head for Durip, a walk of ten miles, three of them perpendicular. At the end of the trail was Father Dan Treanor.

Back down on the road it was possible to continue by jeep to mile 131 where Fathers John O'Sullivan and Hugh O'Rourke lived at Sumprabum. The Irishman from Kerry and the American from Providence, R.I., served a parish that stretched for ninety miles to Putao.

From Sumprabum it was a rough two-day trek to cover the thirty-eight miles to Kajihutu, where Fathers James Feighery and Owen O'Leary had perhaps the most difficult mission assignment in a land of difficult assignments. They spoke lightly of it, as though those twelve-day walks in making the rounds of villages were simply routine. The bishop knew better. Although the new suspension footbridges across the five major rivers helped some, still in the rainy season the mountain paths were slippery and overgrown and the leeches remained a menace.

What a difference, though, twenty years had made up here in the Triangle. Fathers Stuart and Doody had tramped ninety miles looking for a village which would allow them to settle and only Kahihtu would take them in. Then there was not a Catholic in the vast region and now there were 1,500.

Back on the Ledo Road it was possible to travel through the Hukawng Valley by jeep. Fifteen years earlier a report written by the United States Army had called it "the dread Hukawng Valley" because of disease, monsoons, and wild animals.

As for wild animals, the rogue elephants and man-eating tigers had become an increasing problem through the years. When the government took guns away from the Kachins the tribesmen were defenseless against marauding beasts.

Marauding bandits were also a problem. John Howe was especially conscious of them because one armed with a rifle and another with a Sten gun had robbed him and had shot out the tires of his jeep.

On the Ledo Road, at Makawkzup, Fathers James Doody and John Walsh ran a middle school and cared for a widely scattered flock of 3,000 Catholics.

At Tanai, also on the road, Father Kieran Collier opened a new station. He had been pastor at Makawkzup after Father James Stuart started a Catholic community there at the end of the war.

The Columban who lived the greatest distance from the bishop's house in Bhamo was Father James Fisher. Seven hundred miles to the south, in Rangoon, he served as procurator for the Columbans and general secretary of the Catholic hierarchy in Burma. He was assisted by Father Derick Long and by Mr. Fred Machado, a university professor who left teaching to give full-time help to the Columbans.

Bishop Howe could fly from Bhamo to Rangoon within a few hours.

On the way the plane touched down at Momeik, and so if he wanted to see Father Michael Healy he got off and traveled by car to the parish at Pangpau.

The nearest Columbans, of course, were those in Bhamo: Father James Cloonan, bursar; Father Patrick Conneally, pastor; and Fathers David Wall and Colum Murphy, principal and dean of the elementary and secondary schools for boys. The school for girls, staffed by the Franciscan Missionaries of Mary, was located across town.

The nearest parish outside of Bhamo, was the Shan village of Nanhlaing, nine miles away. Father James Foley conducted a school there, and Mother St. Claire, of the Franciscan Missionaries of Mary, operated a dispensary.

"The missionary to the Shans needs heroism of an unusual kind," wrote the superior general, Father Timothy Connolly. "He needs the spirit that will doggedly keep him at his post in spite of abysmal discouragement and difficulties, not the least of which is the feeling, perhaps unconscious but just the same omnipresent, that his fellow missionaries among the Kachins are striding ahead, whereas he is struggling to keep from being engulfed. Fathers Cooney, Foley, and O'Brien are ideal Shan missionaries. To these men my heart went out."

What John Howe learned while visiting the thirty Columbans in Burma encouraged him to write an optimistic report in 1961, six months after becoming a bishop. He recalled that Patrick Usher had arrived twenty-five years earlier to find only 3,000 Catholics in upper Burma, and now there were 28,000.

The report stressed the need to educate more young people native to Burma for the religious life. The supply of priests, sisters, and brothers from abroad could no longer be depended on. He knew that several priests and nuns were standing by waiting to make the trip—their superiors had told him so—but foreigners were not being granted entrance visas. The government of Burma was beginning to close the door.

Twenty-Two

STORYTELLERS

Monsignor Usher had been a great collector of anecdotes, and, fortunately, Bishop Howe enjoyed and encouraged the story-telling tradition. This is indicated in a letter that a Columban wrote home while visiting in the bishop's residence:

"In the big house beside the church, the priests of the mission are all gathered together. They have come from all sides for their annual retreat, which ended yesterday morning. Many have not seen each other for at least a year.

"Most of the yarns they exchange are true and interesting and sometimes wonderful. The rest are still more wonderful, and there is no one who can contradict them."

Missionaries, for instance, collect anecdotes about cooks the way some people collect recipes. A theme of frustration runs through each story. Typical of the *genre* is one told by Father Francis McManamon:

Word ran through the Kachin hills that the priest was looking for a cook, a good cook, and that he needed one badly. A middle-aged Kachin, with a military bearing and an engaging smile, appeared at the door on a day that the pastor was entertaining Father Edmund McGovern.

"Father, I hear you are looking for a good cook. I am the man for the job. I am an ex-army man. I was in Mesopotamia during the First World War. I cooked there. I neither drink, smoke, gamble, nor tell lies. I can cook and I can stand on my head. I do not know English but I can curse fluently in that language, just like an army officer."

Father McGovern lifted a hand in warning and said to Father McManamon. "Don't engage him and don't fix a salary until I have given him a test. I have been here longer than you. I understand these matters."

Father McGovern turned to the Kachin, who stood at attention as he used to in Upper Mesopotamia. The priest from County Cork said, "Now, my good man, stand on your head."

The Kachin stood on his head. He stood on it a second time. Just for good measure he did a little run around the house.

"Let us hear you curse in English like an army officer."

With a good Oxford accent, the Kachin broke into the ordinary, decent swear words of any self-respecting officer. Then he took a deep breath, got a grip on himself, and addressed the gate post as though it were a stupid batman who had failed to polish his officer's boots before parade. What a string of expletives!

Even the priest from County Cork was impressed. He raised his hand with some urgency. The flow came to an abrupt halt.

"You may give him the job. And a good salary. He can stand on his head, as he said. He can curse like an English army officer, as he said. Evidently he does not tell lies. He says he can cook, and I believe him."

Fortunately for Father McGovern, he was far away at breakfast the next morning when the new cook entered from the kitchen on a run and planked down the porridge in the center of the table.

"At least it looked like porridge," said Father McManamon, "but what riveted my attention was the vessel in which it was served. There sat the kitchen saucepan in all the glory of its smoke, soot, and ashes, right in the center of the snow-white table cloth."

Father McManamon and the cook came to an agreement: never again was the saucepan to be seen outside the kitchen. The pastor turned his attention to the porridge, of which he drank a little.

At dinner, chicken was served with the leftover porridge poured over it. When the priest objected, the cook became fatherly: "Eat up, it's just the thing for a growing boy."

From that point on the pastor realized what a thin edge there is between tears and laughter.

"I was no longer master in my house. Cook made a thousand mistakes a day. I can boast that I have known a man who never did one single duty exactly right. I'd get annoyed and then I'd laugh. I couldn't give him the sack. But at the first chance I promoted him to gardener and got a new cook. With a spade and a bit of land he was perfectly happy."

Years later Father McManamon heard the true story of his former cook's military career. He had boiled the officers' shaving water and had heated mash for mules in Upper Mesopotamia. Before long he had been kicked in the head and discharged.

Another cook story was told about Ma Tang who worked for Fathers Daniel McGeown and Patrick Madden. He could really cook but had the serious defect of fancying himself as a musician. During the war he had picked up a bugle which he treasured and blew it every spare moment. That was bad enough during the daylight hours but when he greeted the rising sun each morning the priests began to feel sorry for themselves.

Both missionaries tried blowing the bugle but could not coax a note from it. Their failure encouraged Ma Tang to blow all the more, trumpeting his superiority through the jungle.

The priests began wondering how to give their cook a lesson in humility. Their chance came the day they received a victrola and a stack of records, one of which was a recording of bugle calls: the crack buglers of the Irish Army Band!

Father Madden hid the victrola behind a screen in the far corner of the room. Father McGeown stationed himself with the bugle in the doorway. Ma Tang was preparing a meal in the kitchen.

Suddenly, Ireland's best buglers sent *Reveille* through the Kachin hills. A crash of plates and Ma Tang came flying through the kitchen door. Behold, there was his pastor, standing tall with a silver bugle tight-pressed against bursting lips! The cook's face reflected amazement and rapture.

From the rousing tune of morning call the priest moved to the dignified notes of *General Salute*. From *To the Colors* he progressed to the quiet melodies of *Sundown* and on to the deeply moving *Last Post*.

It just had to happen. His swollen lips failed. He ceased blowing just for a second while the music continued on. A look of scorn came over Ma Tang's face.

Father McGeown burst into laughter. Father Madden joined him. Ma Tang added his voice to the chorus.

From that day forward life was more pleasant around the rectory because the cook spent more time listening than playing. He sat with his ear against the victrola lest he miss even one note. He never learned the name of the record, but he observed the well-known trade mark on the label. So each day he said, "Father, I want to hear the *Listening Dog*."

Father McManamon used to tell a solemn story about the day he thought he might be confronted by Old Nick himself. It happened when a pagan family eleven miles away expressed a wish to become Christian and asked that the priest pay a visit.

On the way, the catechist warned the missionary to be careful because one member of the family, a youth of twenty-one, had the gift of prophecy. He could raise to his lips a five-gallon tin of water and drink it all without lowering the tin. He had raised aloft and juggled a container holding nearly a half-ton of rice.

"He has a harelip. You will know him by that. His name is Ma La. The people consider him possessed by the devil."

Father McManamon stopped in his tracks. "This was my problem in a nutshell: If I retreat I'll have the devil of a conscience; if I advance, I'll have the devil himself."

He advanced. At the house he found nothing unusual. The family gave him a most enthusiastic welcome and seated him by the fireside. They talked of this and that and the priest's eye wandered uneasily in search of Ma La. After about ten minutes the boy put in an appearance and seated himself by the fireside.

"I ventured a few words to him and he answered in a perfectly normal manner. After I had plucked up enough courage we started a long conversation. Nothing seemed too abnormal. True, he was a bit self-conscious and sensitive about his deformity. He probably suffered a little from introspection and depression."

When Ma La departed, the missionary asked his family about all those stories of prophecy and feats of skill and of muscle. All insisted that a few years earlier the boy could drink unusual quantities of water and carry unusual weights. From this they found it easy to credit his powers of prophecy.

Ma La's elder brother, Ma Gam, was working in Lashio, 300 miles from home, when the Japanese invaded Burma in 1942. Ma La prophesied that the Japanese would take Lashio and that Ma Gam would be killed by a truck. So when the Japanese took Lashio everyone in the village took for granted that Ma Gam had also been killed by a truck. Ma La said he had seen it in a vision.

There was much sorrow and weeping. The family held a great funeral feast, having killed three bullocks and several pigs to placate evil *nats* and feed good friends. They buried Ma Gam *in absentia* just as solemnly as if his corpse had been in the coffin.

When the war ended in 1945 who should come walking into the

village but Ma Gam himself. That, however, did not shake anyone's faith in Ma La's special abilities to foretell events.

Ma Gam had married a Catholic girl in Lashio. The two of them induced the rest of the family to accept Catholicism. That is how Father McManamon happened to be sitting by the fireside speaking about a boy's gift of prophecy.

One of Father Rillstone's favorite stories had to do with the curse of the evil eye. While attending a funeral of a local chief, an old woman whispered into the missionary's ear, "We're happy now. The Great Tiger is dead." She went on to list all the aches and pains that the old chief had caused because he had the evil eye.

The Columban chided her for her uncharitable remarks about the dead. As a rebuttal the old woman told of the time the chief had become annoyed with a farmer and before long the farmer's pony dropped dead in front of his house.

At any gathering of Columbans such a story would lead to other evil eye anecdotes. One missionary recalled an experience the Mother Superior of the Franciscan Missionaries of Mary had while attending the sick in a distant village. At the end of the day she started home with six small chickens in a woven bamboo basket, a present from a grateful patient. As she and the girl who had accompanied her walked along a jungle trail, they met an old woman who asked what was in the basket. The nun removed the covering and proudly showed the chickens.

As soon as the curious woman had moved on down the trail, the nun's traveling companion said, "Mother, you shouldn't have let that woman look at your chickens. She has the evil eye. Now all your chickens will die."

The Mother Superior scolded the girl for still harboring such superstitious fancies.

Next morning all of the chickens were dead.

Trial by ordeal is another superstition that finds its way into the Columban repertory of anecdotes. A missionary told of a young girl, engaged to be married, who was accused of stealing a necklace. Since there were no witnesses the village elders called for a trial by ordeal.

They melted lead and told the girl that to prove her innocence she must trail her hand through the bubbling pot. When she refused, the man she was to marry grabbed her wrist and tried to drag her hand through the melted metal. He succeeded in getting only the finger tips to touch the lead.

She screamed. The elders found that some of the lead had stuck to the fingernails. That was enough to convict her.

The girl was branded as a thief and her engagement broken. She had little hope of ever again being engaged. This among the Kachins is tragic because the girls look forward to the security of married life.

In Father Rillstone's village a soldier was accused of stealing another soldier's salary. The platoon sergeant decided to put an end to the shouted accusations and denials by ordering a trial by ordeal.

He poured water into a deep pot and kept it on the fire until it came to a boil. Into the bubbling water he dropped three small lead pellets. One of the soldiers took the hand of the accused, immersed it up to the wrist, then moved it back and forth three times slowly and told him to pick up the three pellets. The accused did it.

The accuser was forced to submit to the same performance, but he was unable to pick up the pellets. So the accused was declared innocent.

The hands of both boys became swollen and started to turn black. At the hospital the Franciscan Sisters were able to save them.

One of Father Bernard Way's favorite anecdotes was about how he became the father of the bride, and, in time, a grandfather. It happened because Monica, a teacher in his parish, was an orphan.

When Monica's wedding approached, the parishioners decided that the pastor should represent the bride when time came to dicker with the parents of the groom. He must see to it that the wedding was a splendid affair.

"I entertain the greatest respect for Oriental prowess in bargaining," said Father Way. "So I hastily assembled a team of experts to help me face the boys from over the hill. Some kerosene cans of rice whiskey were brought in. The palaver was about to begin."

The suitor's representatives brought a large gong as a gift for the father of the bride. His four experts went over it, holding it to their ears, and commenting on its size. They found it too small. Only eight handspans. What a pity! Only eight. Even if it were ten, this would be an insult to the father of the bride.

The point was conceded. At a later date a bigger gong would be brought to the *Jan Kabe*. Round one went to the father of the bride.

Next the silks. Father Way discerned a surge of suppressed admiration. The word traveled around in whispers. But spoken aloud was a grudging, "The silks are passable."

The suitor's party had brought a buffalo. "Where are the cows?"

"But wait till you see the pony that goes with the buffalo."

The pony drew only scorn: Over at the knees, spavined, long in the teeth.

The demand continued for at least another buffalo and a few cows.

The gesticulating and arguing went on and on until Father Way fell asleep in the chair. Monica awakened him when she brought in bamboo tubes of beer to fortify both sides. Only night and weariness brought an end to the proceedings. The bride's team withdrew congratulating itself on its victories.

The wedding ceremony was the only restful lull in the whole affair. Right after it hostilities broke out anew, this time on the question of retinue.

The groom's parents wanted two girls and two boys to accompany the bride. Monica had other ideas. She wasn't going to travel that long distance, through many villages, looking like a poor orphan. If the husband's family couldn't pay for a large retinue, why did they come for her at all. It was finally agreed that she should have five maids-of-honor and five gentlemen-in-waiting, with a couple of older people as chaperones.

The head bargainer of the groom's party made a speech. He told Father Way that he had the consolation of having the pony to carry the loads that Monica would have carried and that the gong would take the place of her voice.

At this point in the story Bernard Way's fellow Columbans pointed out that he seemed to be on the receiving end of things. What did he give in return?

"You talk as though I am the grasping Shylock in this drama. Let me remind you that among the Kachins the father of the bride equips his daughter with a dowry, and bridal costume, silver earrings, necklaces, bangles, and all."

And so the stories go. They range from cooks to evil eyes and floods, on and on to rogue elephants and man-eating tigers. Unfortunately, the Columbans have mainly an oral tradition, and not many of their yarns are committed to paper. Since the stories are passed along by word of mouth they do, in time, die out. Many have been lost beyond recall. Once gone they are as irretrievable as yesterday.

Twenty-Three

SISTERS COME TO HELP

The evening angelus was ringing in Rangoon when five Columban sisters arrived at the Good Shepherd convent on Saturday, June 6, 1947. The convent, once beautiful, now stood amid the rubble of war—a shambles. More than thirty years later Sister Ita O'Mahony recalled the sight:

"Rangoon had nothing of the glamour of the East. There was devastation and wreckage everywhere. Poverty seemed rampant. It was a dismal setting for one starting a new mission."

The next problem was to get to Myitkyina, 1,000 miles to the north. The British were still in Burma, and so the sisters hoped that they might hitch a ride on an army plane; after all, they had come out from Liverpool on a British troopship, the *Worcestershire*.

For a week they hoped and prayed, and finally at five o'clock one morning they climbed aboard the last British plane scheduled to leave Rangoon for Myitkyina. Arriving at noon on a hot and humid day, they found that their new home was a small brick structure not substantial enough to keep out the rain when it comes down the way it does in upper Burma. The schoolhouse was another discouraging sight, a frail bamboo structure that was supposed to hold 120 pupils.

It took the children to bring a great lift to the hearts of the five new missionaries. "The children of Burma are beautiful in their simplicity," said Sister Ita. "There they were—Burmans, Chinese, Indians and Kachins. For me the Kachins were a people for whom God had a special predilection. They were ready to receive the faith. By this time the Columban Fathers had a vast apostolate in the villages of the jungle."

When school began on July 1, it was evident at a glance that the bamboo structure was no longer adequate. "Children from the jungle clamoured for education," recalled Sister Ita. "And all literally thirsted to know more about the faith. They were 'new' Catholics and were our great apostolate.

"All five sisters were busy teaching and making home visitations. It was a great help when Sister Mary Colmcille came from the Philippines and Sister Mary Oliver from Shanghai."

A boarding school was the first priority. So many children wanted to come to Myitkyina from villages a hundred or more miles away that after eight months the Columban Sisters opened a boarding school for thirty pupils. Although fees for board and tuition totaled only $1.80 a month, the sisters managed to make a go of it because things were still cheap.

"At the rate the work was growing," said Sister Andrew, another of the pioneers, "we realized that more and more buildings would be needed. Money was scarce, and so we decided to send out appeals, mostly to the United States where the response was most generous. Eventually, we began to build. In 1956 we saw our dreams take shape: the convent, day school, and boarding school."

While dreams took shape, so did new problems. The government, not wanting any more foreigners coming into Burma, began to refuse visas. Because of this new policy it was not possible to replace three sisters lost to the mission: Sisters Colmcille and Oliver had to return to Ireland because of poor health, and Sister Celestine, the youngest of the group, died in 1954 of cerebral malaria after only a week of illness.

Although it seemed that no new sisters would be arriving, this did not stop Bishop Howe from dreaming of a clinic. His diocese had a number of dispensaries where ordinary ailments were treated with ordinary patent medicine, but a clinic was another matter. He realized that he would need sisters especially trained in medical skills to plan such a building.

Out of the blue, Sister Madeleine was allowed to enter Burma. As a nurse she had worked in Scotland before joining the Columban Sisters. Later she went to Hong Kong to work for three years in a sanatorium operated by the Columban Sisters and from there to Korea to help Archbishop Harold Henry, a Columban, establish a clinic.

Next Sister Dorothea arrived from Hong Kong. She had trained at St. Vincent's hospital, Dublin, and after graduation had done postgraduate work in the Brompton Chest Hospital in London.

The Mother General of the Columbans promised that Sisters Fintan and Kieran would soon be on the way and that a sister physician would be available before long. So things looked bright when construction of the clinic began toward the end of 1962.

Bishop Howe recalls: "We chose a site beside a village called Manbang, sixty-five miles from Myitkyina on the Ledo Road, the road to India. The village is in a vast plain that was being rapidly settled and cultivated by Kachins from the surrounding hills and from the neighboring Shan states. This populated area showed every sign of growth and seemed the right place for a clinic.

"It was also a suitable location for a priest's residence. I appointed Father Frank McManamon as chaplain to the sisters; I wanted to place him where he might take some of the burden off the two parishes already in the area. Father Kieran Collier was in Tanai, sixty miles toward India; and Fathers John Walsh and Robert O'Rourke were in Makawkzup, twenty miles away in the direction of Myitkyina."

The sisters moved to Manbang in October of 1963. "It was a beautiful scenic spot." Sister Ita recalls, "At night tigers peered at us in the dark. Monkeys, with their not-too-melodious chatter, awakened us each morning."

No sooner had the sisters arrived than they began to dream of a mobile clinic, one that might operate up and down the length of the Ledo Road. These hopes were never realized, though, because when the Burmans and the Kachins began to war with each other, the sisters got caught in the crossfire.

On Columban's Day in 1963, Sisters Andrew and Ita were returning to Manbang from Myitkyina with Father Walsh at the wheel of the jeep when they ran into an ambush. The three of them crouched for hours at the edge of the road with bullets whistling all about.

Although they came through that close call unharmed, Father Walsh would soon die trying to be of help to the sisters. It happened on the Monday of Holy Week, 1964; he set off on his motorcycle for Mogaung to buy some supplies for the clinic. When he failed to return to his parish at Mogokzup by nightfall, his colleague, Father Bob O'Rourke, began to worry about him and set out for Mogaung to inquire as to his safety.

Four miles from Mogaung, Father O'Rourke came upon a search party standing around Father Walsh's body lying face down in a shallow grave with his rosary beads under his face. There were two bullet wounds in the head and one in the chest. On his right leg there were three gashes, apparently inflicted by a *dah,* a long knife commonly used in Burma. The Kachins and the Burmans blamed the murder on each other.

Father Walsh's body was taken to Myitkyina where it was buried in the town cemetery on the morning of Holy Thursday. In recalling the Requiem Mass, Bishop Howe said: "The first relief we got from the awful shock of his death came when we priests spent the evening in Myitkyina recalling some of his many stories. How he unfailingly cheered us with his bubbling good humor and inexhaustible anecdotes! I thought that night that this is the way he would have wanted us to remember him."

By now it was evident that the sisters would have to abandon their clinic. "Things were worsening every day," said Sister Ita. "Bishop Howe thought we ought to get out. That was easier said than done. We were completely cut off from Myitkyina. We had to get permission from both armies. After long deliberations, we were allowed to take a Land Rover driven by Father McManamon.

"After Mass on April 30, we bade good-bye to the wailing people. That night brought us safely to Father Stuart's village, empty except for a few cattle. We slept in an empty house, on the bamboo floor, and had Mass there the next day. We traveled through many an obstacle; a passage had to be cut through the jungle. At Makawkzup, Father Walsh's house was empty. Soldiers told us we could take the jeep no further."

The priest and two sisters decided to walk to the railroad twenty miles from there. On the way they passed a Burmese army camp; a sentry halted them, curious as to what the unlikely trio was up to.

"Providence was on our side," recalls Sister Andrew. "The man in charge had been a friend of ours. He took us to the camp and served us tea as we sat atop guns. He offered to send us by army truck to Myitkyina but we were afraid to travel with soldiers; we might be fired on.

"Just then a truck came along, loaded with building materials, on its way to Myitkyina. The driver, an Indian boy, said that two of his sisters were pupils in our schools and he would be glad to give us a ride. We sat on the load of timber and not once did it dawn on us that we were uncomfortable. Along the way the sentries waved us on; they had been given the order to do so."

"At six in the evening we arrived at Myitkyina," said Sister Ita. "We were greeted by Bishop Howe. A Mass of thanksgiving was offered almost immediately.

"A week later a soldier arrived carrying a lunette that he had found in Father Walsh's house. The sacred host was in it. He gave it to me and said, 'I felt it was precious.' "

The Columban sisters from the clinic settled down to school work, excepting Sister Madeleine Lillis who went to Korea. Things seemed to be going well until March of 1965 when they were suddenly surrounded by soldiers and the officer in command announced that the government was taking over the school.

"We never again entered the school," said Sister Andrew. "But we stayed on in the convent and went out among the people every day teaching religion. By this time quite a number of our pupils had entered an order of native sisters in southern Burma and were ready to come back to take over where we left off. But not in the school, of course."

Sister Andrew was referring to the Sisters of St. Francis Xavier. They opened their first convent near Myitkyina in 1962 and at this writing have five convents in the diocese.

Losing the clinic and school were severe blows to the Columban Sisters, but the worst of all came a year later when they were expelled from Burma. More about this later.

"In June of 1966 we bade farewell to the people we loved," said Sister Ita. "I felt my heart would break."

"It was harder to leave Burma than it was to leave Ireland," said another of the sisters.

Twenty-Four

"MYIT SU AI"

At the end of the war, just after being released from thirty-four months of internment, Fathers Bernard Way and Lawrence Mc-Mahon were visiting some of the thirty-five villages in Father Way's parish of Ting Sing. In a village called Lunghkat the priests met Sara Zinghtung Gam, the head catechist of the area, and his wife and six children. One of the children, Grawng, was six years old.

Thirty years later, Father McMahon searched his memory trying to recall the boy, Grawng, but he could not. It made him realize how it is possible to meet someone who will, in time, be important in your life, and be completely oblivious of it, and he realized also how unpredictable is the future.

"I do remember meeting Grawng's parents," said Father McMahon. "We became friends for life. The catechist hadn't been highly educated but he had an innate dignity which gained him the respect of all.

"And Grawng's grandfather also stood out as a man of great dignity. In Kachin such a man is said to be *myit su ai.* It's difficult to find a single word in English to express its exact meaning, but it includes wise and prudent and having dignity. Grandfather Zinghtung was all of that."

Years later Grawng told how his grandfather happened to become a Catholic: After much thought the old man decided to follow the example of some of his neighbors and forsake the cult of placating the *nat-ni,* evil spirits, and to worship God. He found himself wooed by Baptists and Catholics alike.

Grandfather Zinghtung knew that Lunghkat was visited periodically by both Catholic priest and Baptist minister. He decided to accept the next to arrive, and when the priest did, Zinghtung had himself and his family enrolled as catechumens.

The grandson, Grawng, grew up to become the first Kachin priest and bishop. His two sisters were members of the Franciscan Missionaries of Mary, and his aunt and other relatives joined the Sisters of St. Francis Xavier.

When Father Way left Ting Sing, Father McMahon remained as pastor for many years. Lunghkat was one of his favorite villages. "As we say in the Gauri vernacular, which the Lunghkat people speak: '*I kahtawng*—it's our village.' "

When Sara Zinghtung Gam was stricken with cancer and died suddenly, Father McMahon happened to be in Bhamo where Grawng attended boarding school. "I can still remember his expression of shock and bewilderment as he set off home for the funeral. His mother, Anastasia Lazum Htu, was now a young widow with six children and a child on the way, a boy that died shortly after birth. Anastasia was a valiant woman, then as always."

During his seminary days Grawng spent part of his vacation helping Father McMahon train altar boys, conduct choir practice, and supervise church decorations. The pastor of Ting Sing knew he would miss the young man after ordination.

In 1961, 15,000 Catholics gathered from every part of the Kachin State for the dedication of the Bhamo central church. At the conclusion of the three-day ceremony, Archbishop Knox, apostolic delegate to Burma, addressed the huge congregation in English. Grawng, then twenty-two, stood by as interpreter, giving a flawless translation into Kachin.

When Grawng was ordained a priest in 1965 Grandfather Zinghtung was still much in evidence. At one of the general meetings, called a *zuph-pawng,* the old man was invited to the speakers' platform. He hobbled up, bent almost double under his eighty-plus years, and began to speak.

He told the hushed audience that he was glad to see his grandson a priest. Then he paused for a moment and cried out: "And I hope that some day he will become a bishop!"

He was answered by a roar of laughter and delighted applause. The old man still is *myit su ai* they said, and so is the grandson, far beyond his years.

After ordination Father Grawng taught for several years at the major seminary in Rangoon before returning to his diocese to take up pastoral work and administrative duties under Bishop Howe. The bishop said that when he ordained Paul Grawng the first Kachin priest he little dreamed that eleven years later, April 3, 1976, he would ordain him the first Kachin bishop.

The ceremony was the highlight of the three-day centennial observing the founding of the church in upper Burma. For the celebration they came 17,000 strong out of the Kachin hills, through the valleys and across the plains.

They traveled to Myitkyina by every means of transportation—cart, truck, train, boat, airplane. Thousands had to walk, often for several days. One group of 500 from Father Hugh O'Rourke's old parish in the far north hiked for eight days through the Triangle Mountains. From Bhamo 450 traveled the easy way, by chartered plane.

On the first night, a community penitential and absolution service prepared the visitors to participate in the liturgical celebrations. For each of the next three days more than 7,000 received Holy Communion.

A Kachin priest wrote a special centenary hymn, set to traditional music by an Anglican university graduate. It was sung for Mass each day, led by a choir of 200, accompanied by flutes, cymbals, and gongs.

An unusual feature of the celebration was the traditional *Manau*, the victory dance. Bishop Grawng, the six visiting bishops, the priests, and sisters all joined in. It was held in the dancing ring, a large area enclosed by a lattice fence of spliced bamboo and decorated with streamers stretched from fence to totemlike poles in the middle of the ring. The poles were decorated with multicolored curves and spirals to indicate the pattern of the dance. There were some adaptations: a huge cross was set in the middle of the posts and the six leaders each carried a small cross instead of a sword.

After Bishop Grawng had blessed the ring, a hundred dancers began the movements to the beat of many gongs, the wailing of bamboo flutes, and a song that told of what had happened during the church's 100 years in these hills.

On the second day, Bishop Grawng ordained two Kachin priests. To celebrate that occasion, a "short" concert began at 8:00 p.m. and lasted until 2:30 the next morning.

The feast committee ordered thirty-seven buffaloes—all were slaughtered and eaten—twenty-five tons of rice, mounds of vegetables, and piles of firewood for cooking. Each day rations were distributed to 17,000 people.

The parishioners of Myitkyina and neighboring parishes built the

Mandat, a temporary church for the occasion. The structure, 195 feet long and 135 feet wide, was constructed of bamboo and thatch without a nail being used. The army loaned tarpaulins and brought in water for cooking and drinking. Government officials in Rangoon, Myitkyina, and Bhamo arranged for special plane, boat, and train transport.

The *Mandat* was dismantled and every sign of the celebration cleared away in less than a week after the feast. Most of the work was done by 200 students who set up a youth camp for that purpose immediately after the celebration.

Bishop Howe stood in awe at the way things were accomplished. "There was a time just two weeks before the opening date when it really looked as if we could not hold it on anything like the scale we had planned. The problems seemed to be insoluble. But during the last week one difficulty after another disappeared. Miraculously, we found ourselves gathered together at last with a much bigger crowd than expected.

"We had been praying for a year that our heavenly Father would use the occasion to renew and strengthen our faith. He granted our prayer."

At the time, Bishop Howe was aware that he had only ten Columbans left in Burma and that, because of government rules, no more could be sent in. The average age was sixty, some struggled with health problems, and none had had a vacation away from the demanding terrain and climate of the Kachin hills for ten or fifteen years.

Ten energetic young Kachin priests were there to carry on the work. Yet many more were needed to staff the twenty parishes and mission stations. New parishes were needed to care for the 60,000 Catholics in the Kachin State, an area the size of Kentucky.

Bishop Howe thought often of what foresight Monsignor Usher had shown when, in 1950, he told his priests he wanted to send some boys to the minor seminary in Mandalay. Many heads shook in disagreement.

Six Kachin boys went to the seminary in Mandalay in 1951. Within a few months five returned home, but Paul Grawng stayed on. By the time he was ordained a bishop ten other Kachins had become priests. Nine Kachins were in the major seminary, sixty in the minor, and sixty nuns were at work in the diocese.

Shortly after the ceremony Bishop Howe and his new auxiliary, Bishop Grawng, reviewed the situation in the diocese: of the 60,000

Catholics, three-quarters of them only occasionally see a priest or receive the sacraments. For example, Father Hugh O'Rourke's old parish of Sumprabum is such a minidiocese that the Kachin pastor, reaching a remote mission station for the first time in several months, had to hear confessions all night long.

The two bishops decided that, instead of tying down all the young Kachin priests to parishes, they would organize them into teams with catechists and sisters, and in that way they could cover a larger area more effectively.

"We've always had catechists, of course," said Bishop Howe, "but in 1972 we adopted a plan to train more and to involve the laity in other ways, too. Now we have over 200 catechists. Many have taken the intensive two-year course we set up. They're doing a wonderful job, but they are constantly on the go. Some have as many as twenty villages to care for.

"For the time being we have converted our catechists' center into a place to train Christian village leaders. In six months they get an intensive course in conducting liturgical prayer services. Besides being prayer leaders they will be 'life leaders.' By that I mean they'll build up their villages economically as well as spiritually; they'll show their people how to live a better life.

"The lay people are getting more involved in administering the parishes. The Catholic Lay Association collected funds to build the temporary church and buy food for Bishop Grawng's ordination."

The young bishop assured Bishop Howe that the Kachin priests and people want the Columbans to stay as long as possible. "Every year you stay," he said, "gains precious time for those of us who follow."

As they spoke Bishop Howe kept thinking that there are twenty-five years of struggle ahead for the young church in the Kachin hills. It is not just a matter of needing priests, sisters, cathechists, and educators; a greater need, for the moment, is the blessing of peace. War and rebellion have plagued many parts of the country ever since Burma achieved independence from the British in 1948.

Things were quiet in the Kachin State until about 1960, when the Kachins sought complete independence rather than accept a limited autonomy within the Union of Burma. The result has been continual strife.

As always, the ordinary village people are caught in the middle and are suspected by both sides. Sometimes entire villages have been deserted, with terrified people fleeing to the jungle. During intensive guerrilla fighting one of the larger villages was burnt out three times.

Planting and harvesting of rice, the staple food, are impeded by the fighting. For instance, many people have been moved to larger centers and now must hike fifteen miles to tend their tiny rice fields.

A shortage of food leads to malnutrition and an array of diseases. With a scarcity of rice the economy is tilted out of balance until other essential commodities become harder to find and are priced out of reason.

"The war in the Kachin State gets no international publicity," said Bishop Howe, "but it is very real and tragic for the people there."

All these troubles were in his thoughts the day he consecrated Paul Zinghtung Grawng a bishop. He felt that the young man, only thirty-seven years old, would need all the talents God had given him. And yet he felt encouraged because it is evident that the new bishop, like his father and grandfather, is *myit su ai.*

Twenty-Five

TIME OF TORMENT

The decade of the sixties was a distressful one for the Columbans. The guerrilla war, a torment for many years, became a real agony in 1962 when the Kachins revolted against the government of the Union of Burma. The missionaries felt vulnerable because they were foreigners living in a sensitive area along the China border, and most touchy of all was the fact that their parishioners were mainly Kachins, a tribe now taking up arms for a separate state.

From the beginning the Columbans decided not to take sides. The issues were too complex for a foreigner to see objectively, even a foreigner who had lived in the land for thirty years.

Bishop Howe let it be known, especially among Catholics, that the priests would not become involved in politics. The missionaries were so faithful to this policy that no one ever accused them of interfering. Everyone seemed satisfied that they were doing only what they had come to do, preach the gospel.

The most tragic incident, of course, came in March of 1963 when Father John Walsh was murdered. His colleagues had to listen and say nothing while accusations and counteraccusations flew back and forth among the warring groups. All they could do was mourn the death of a man they had held in high regard.

When the revolutionary council took over the government in 1962, it decreed that if foreign missionaries left the country for any reason whatever, they would not be given reentry visas. This was a blow to the Columbans, who normally went home every six years for a year of rest and medical treatment. Consequently, the number of Columbans decreased and the health and strength of those who remained deteriorated. With each year the building up of the church in Burma was becoming more of a burden.

A government decree in 1965 presented the Columbans with another critical situation. On April 1, all private schools were nationalized. Of the 102 high and middle schools taken over, 49 were Catholic and the rest were administered by groups from other religions.

Years later, Father Colum Murphy recalled that morning in April when he was helping clean the school in Bhamo and was told that it belonged to the Columbans no longer.

"It was a blow," he said. "We had to adjust ourselves to carry on without schools. The sisters in particular adapted themselves admirably, going around visiting the people in their homes and organizing catechism classes in private homes. The work of the missionary was getting harder and harder."

When the schools were nationalized they lost the religious atmosphere in which boys and girls might study while waiting to become priests or nuns. Years earlier Monsignor Usher had shown foresight when he insisted on opening a minor seminary even though many heads shook in disagreement.

"Yes, I know the time is not right," the quiet-spoken monsignor had said, "but unless we can build up a local clergy here, our work will have no permanent success."

The priests had pointed out that Kachins, even those who became Catholic, hold to the tradition of their race that it is the duty of the sons and daughters to marry and to provide many grandchildren. If not, who will look after the sick and the aged when they are no longer able to work in the fields? This is a legitimate fear, the missionaries had argued, for people who know nothing of pensions and Social Security.

The monsignor had nodded. Yes, he admitted all of this, but all the same he started a small seminary in 1950 in Mogok, and appointed Father Magee rector. The site was chosen chiefly because it is a cool, healthy, quiet place, and because the Columbans owned two small buildings there where Father Trainor was pastor.

Patrick Usher used to insist that the two years a student spent in Magok must be pleasant ones: "He may come from a simple mountain home and it is important that his first step should not be difficult or in any way alarming. He will not have to go a very great distance and he will be with companions of his own race under a priest who knows his language and the mentality of his people. Afterward, having had some training in the ways of seminaries, he will be ready for the subsequent steps."

The next step was to Maymyo, sixty miles to the south. In British times this town, 4,000 feet above sea level, was the holiday residence of the governor of Burma and of lesser luminaries. Some of its glory had departed by the time the seminarians arrived, but it was still a pleasant place, cool and quiet, with lovely scenery. The seminary at Maymyo was staffed by the priests from Mandalay and was under direction of Patrick Usher's friend, Bishop Faliere.

The final step was to the major seminary in Rangoon.

After nationalization of the schools this system was no longer practicable. So Bishop Howe took an old house in Myitkyina, one formerly occupied by priests, and turned it into a boarding school for boys who wanted to study for the priesthood.

Each day the boys walked to the local government school and after class hours were given such religious training as could be fitted in. A similar arrangement was made for girls who wished to become nuns. Although at the start the system was less than satisfactory, from such a modest beginning Father O'Sullivan developed a large building with adequate facilities.

Another shattering blow came in 1965 when the government decreed that all foreigners with temporary stay permits could not have their permits renewed and so would have to leave the country before the end of 1966.

From the time Burma became independent in 1948, the government had treated all religions with tolerance and respect. Right from the beginning, however, the new regime placed some restrictions on the admission into the country of new missionaries: They would have to have certain academic qualifications and would be given temporary visas. Only those who had been in Burma before independence would be able to retain their permanent visas.

As far back as 1957 Monsignor Usher had written: "No new priests are coming to join us. Permission for them to enter the country has not been forthcoming in spite of our best efforts to obtain it. The last considerable batch arrived as far back as 1946. Only two, Fathers Conneally and Walsh, have been admitted since then and these two are restricted to school work; they are forbidden to do ordinary mission work.

"In those eleven years our losses through death and ill health have averaged one a year. The remainder of us are eleven years older, in an environment where every year counts. For us the mountains seem steeper each year and the climate heavier. We admit that youth has its points and would welcome a sprinkling of it."

Although Monsignor Usher complained about not getting more missionaries he did not accuse the government of intolerance. He did not doubt the sincerity of U Nu, who spoke of the church in glowing terms at the National Eucharistic Congress in Rangoon in 1956:

"I have pleasure in stating that since I came to power I have noticed the continual respect the Catholic Church has earned for three principles: showing loyalty to the Burmese Union and its government; refraining from taking part in politics; and busying itself with religion and nothing else.

"It has been the ideal church for the Burmese Union. Burmese Catholics have powerfully contributed to its history. I am happy that I have been given this opportunity to thank them all. The missionaries have done excellent work, especially in the fields of education and social assistance."

These were not empty words, as was shown two years later when eight Columbans were allowed to enter the country with temporary permits.

When those with temporary stay permits were asked to leave and when the schools were nationalized, the Columbans saw none of this as anti-Christian intolerance. It had to do with the government wanting to gain control of social structure, hoping to develop the culture of the people while freeing them from foreign influence.

No matter what the reason for the government action, 1966 was a dark one for the missionaries. Eight of the youngest priests, eight Columban sisters, two De La Salle brothers and four Franciscan Missionaries of Mary departed, leaving Bishop Howe with sixteen Columban priests and two Kachin priests, Father Paul Grawng and Thomas Nawhkum Naw.

On the day the first group of Columbans departed, May 21, 1966, one of them remarked: "Monsignor Usher may well have sensed as far back as 1946 what was on the road ahead. It was then he organized the Catholic Committee." This committee of laymen worked with the priest to organize retreats, helped catechists with instruction, and developed a diocesan financial fund. A church of the laity was being developed in the Kachin hills sixteen years before the Second Vatican Council.

Thirty years after the Catholic Committee had been organized Father Foley, in a report to the Society of St. Columban in 1975, admitted that the committee "certainly had its growing pains and provided us with more than its share of problems." He concluded that in spite of all of this, the plan was a good one. "We must go on record as saying that the seeds were sown for the vast network of Catholic action which flourishes in the diocese today."

Because of Monsignor Usher's foresight in starting the Catholic Committee, Bishop Howe was able, in 1972, to convene a successful diocesan synod in Myitkyina. Laymen, 235 in all, met for a week to accept new responsibilities. They decided how they might conduct Sunday services, arrange for religious instruction in villages without a resident or visiting catechist, collect church revenue, select scholarship candidates for the university, elect their own Catholic Action leaders, and accept complete responsibility for feasts which play such an important role in the religious life of the people.

At the time of the Synod, Father Kelleher observed how attitudes had changed within the church since the Columbans had reached Burma in 1936: "In the old days our mission attitudes were rather colonial. Our Catholic communities were cut off from the rest and became something of a ghetto. We did not have that outgoing spiritual mind or attitude that I think we have now. We have become more a part of the people and our attitudes toward non-Christians and Buddhists have changed. I think we are more acceptable to the people now because the triumphalism is gone."

This growth of responsibility among laymen was all well and good, but how much would the image of the church change now that the government had taken away schools, hospitals, leper colonies, and orphanages? The missionaries felt that although Catholics were less than one percent of the population, still the church's organizations had given a visibility and an influence that was well beyond statistics.

The superior general of the Paris Foreign Missions, Monsignor Queguiner, sensed this when visiting his priests in Burma in 1970. In a report to his society he said: "The church in Burma is bearing extraordinary testimony to Christ because it is one of the few missions in the world where the church possesses neither hospitals, nor schools, nor many other social works, since they were taken over by the government in 1965. As a consequence, the church lives and develops only inasmuch as she is the church—with the simple force of the Holy Spirit, who acts through her members. No matter how you look at it, the church in Burma is extremely alive."

Twenty-Six

THE DECISION TO LEAVE

Bishop Howe remembers the centenary as an occasion of joy tempered with sadness. There was joy when Paul Grawng was consecrated a bishop, and when he, in turn, ordained two Kachin priests, Joseph Labang Tu and Peter Maw, and when thousands gathered with them to celebrate the hundredth anniversary of the coming of Catholicism to those hills.

Up from Rangoon for the occasion, Marie Nyun, the wife of a Buddhist, said that the ceremonies brought her a bittersweet pang. She felt as though she belonged and yet she was on the outside looking in. "The faith and devotion of the simple hill people, so evident in their prayers, were a reflection of our faith brought a century ago by the French Fathers and extended by the Columbans.

"I walked through the spacious grounds in a haze of gratitude to God," she continued. "There is a quality about some moments in life that catches the heart and makes you wish that time could stand still. Amid all of the rejoicing I realized the poignant fact that the Columbans would soon be withdrawing.

"I know that this is the principal aim of all missionaries: to build up the native clergy and then leave. Still I cannot be reconciled to the fact, at least not yet. These warmhearted priests and good sisters have been, for a number of years, my good friends and teachers. They have encountered soul-testing problems which they had to solve not only as religious but as sorely tried human beings.

"From them we have learned not to sneer and rage, but to be lighthearted and joyful even when we suffer in earnest. They gave us the wisdom of acceptance, the will and resilience to push on.

"What a wrench it will be for us when the remaining few shall bid us farewell forever. It will be for me, as the French say, *'mourir un peu.'* Yes, all of us will die a little."

The sadness that Bishop Howe felt is very well brought out in that letter of Marie Nyun's. He felt it even more a year later when he handed over the diocese formally to Bishop Grawng. On that day, April 24, 1977, when ten Columbans joined ten Kachin priests at concelebrating the Eucharistic sacrifice, everyone was aware that this would be the last time that they would all gather at the altar.

Afterward a two-day seminar was held for catechists and lay leaders. At the closing session, a catechist from Momauk, Sara N. Htoiwa, made an emotional appeal for the Columbans to stay: "It is not just for the help you would give us, but it is also because we don't want to be separated from you."

Time and again the people begged Bishop Howe to stay, and time and again he explained the situation. He was touched by their pleas, but managed to control his emotions until the farewell concert when he thanked them all, and the Lord, for the good things received during his thirty-six years in Burma. He could no longer keep back the tears. "I was relieved when they flowed."

What Bishop Howe had to explain was the decision reached in 1972 when Father Richard Steinhilber, the superior general, came to Rangoon. Since he could not get permission to go to the Kachin State, all the remaining Columbans came down to Rangoon to discuss the future of the Burma mission.

The assembly decided on a five-year plan of withdrawal beginning with 1976. This gave them something definite to work toward and encouraged them to train more lay people, especially catechists. Each priest was aware that soon their parishioners' lives as Catholics would be mainly in the hands of laymen.

In recalling this meeting Bishop Howe said: "One or two of the priests had some misgivings about the plan. They felt we were running away. But the plan went through. We would be officially withdrawing within five years. After 1976, each priest would be free to stay by volunteering on a yearly basis but with the permission and approval of the director, Father Foley, and the bishop. That was made very clear in the document drawn up by Father Steinhilber and Father Foley.

"At the meeting in Rangoon we estimated we would have ten Kachin priests by 1976. And 60,000 Catholics. One priest for every 6,000. And that in difficult territory. Up and down. You have to be young for that work.

"Of the Columbans left we knew that most would stay for a while after 1976. Every year counts in building a local church. The older ones could take care of the old parishes on the plains—Bhamo, Myitkyina, Momauk. That would save them from traveling the hills.

"We left Rangoon after that meeting with the superior general, determined to train enough prayer leaders to put one in each village. Catechists visit a lot of villages but they are not *of* the village. Our prayer leaders would be 'life leaders.' Teach the people how to live. We would train them for that during a special six months' course in the catechist school. They would build up the people economically as well as spiritually.

"I personally felt we should stay after 1976, *provided* we had the health and would not become an extra burden on the Kachin priests. And *provided* we were not an obstacle to them who have ideas, good ideas, about new pastoral methods. Paul Grawng was already showing this in Myitkyina. He had his own way of doing things.

"There was one way we were not giving a proper lead to our young priests. Our standard of living was different from theirs, and they followed it. Ours, far from luxurious, was definitely higher than that found in upper Burma. One advantage of all of us leaving in 1976 would be to get them to live in a way in keeping with the standard of their own people. They were aware of this problem too."

Bishop Howe often asked himself how the church of Myitkyina diocese would finance itself after the Columbans were gone. He talked about this with his confreres. As a result Father Foley, the Columban director in Burma, sent the following recommendation to the General Chapter of the Society of St. Columban held from October 4 to December 8, 1976, in the Philippines.

"Because of the financial difficulties which could arise in the Myitkyina diocese after the necessary Columban withdrawal, the Burma Convention respectfully requests the General Chapter to recommend that the society would give some financial help, more especially for the years immediately following the withdrawal. Further, we would like to suggest that this help be in the form of a definite annual figure at the disposal of the bishop only."

As a result of this recommendation, the Society of St. Columban gives Bishop Grawng the same amount it gave to Bishop Howe, $40,000 a year to take care of the expenses of the diocese. In 1978 it sent an additional $40,000 to relocate families whose crops had been destroyed for two consecutive years by rats. This money came from benefactors who have helped the Columbans in their work for the past sixty-two years.

Additional help comes from Europe. The Society for the Propagation of the Faith in Rome gives $40,000 a year toward the running of the diocese. The Society of Peter the Apostle in Rome gave $8,000 for support of the minor seminary. The Society for the Propagation of the Faith in Aachen gives financial help for the training and support of catechists.

In Sunday collections the parishioners of upper Burma contribute about $20,000 a year. From these statistics it is evident that the diocese of Myitkyima is a long way from being self-supporting.

After the Rangoon meeting in 1972, Bishop Howe wanted more than ever to ordain a Kachin bishop. He felt it would be a gesture of the confidence the Columbans had in the Kachins.

"I asked the apostolic delegate, Archbishop Cassidy, if I might hand over the diocese to a Kachin bishop and become his auxiliary. He could stay in Myitkyina. The church was growing more in that area of the diocese. I could stay in Bhamo, over a hundred miles from Myitkyina, where there was not so much development.

"The apostolic delegate said that it was unheard of. In his usual frankness he said I could be an obstacle in the path of the new Kachin bishop. I might be interfering, without being aware of it, and that would cause pain and trouble in the diocese. That's a fact that has to be taken into account."

That Bishop Howe was justified in his confidence in Bishop Grawng has been proved by the record of the initiatives he took during the two years from his installation on April 24, 1977, until the departure of the last three Columbans on July 2, 1979.

Immediately upon taking up office the young bishop called all his Kachin confreres to a week-long convention at Myitkyina. Before going on to discuss diocesan policy he appealed to his priests to mold and fashion their lives after the example and teaching of Christ, reminding them that success in the apostolate depended on this. Then he outlined the problems that confronted them and suggested new ways of solving them. After much serious discussion they came up with three major resolutions:

1. Emphasis would be laid upon the "group approach" to the apostolate rather than the traditional method of the "individual approach."
2. In future the priest would move out into an area accompanied by sisters, catechists, lay leaders, and youth leaders. On reaching a selected district they would divide into smaller groups. Each group would then set up a center for instruction in Christian doctrine and practice, remaining there until the new converts had received a solid grounding in Christian faith, doctrine and way of living. Then the groups would come together for the reception of Baptism and Confirmation and the Eucharist if they were adults. The priest and his team would then move on to another district.
3. To reach out into hitherto unexplored territory on the borders of China and India. Here again the approach would be used, but the team in this instance would not be accompanied by a priest, neither would it be possible to engage in weeks of instruction.

This third resolution was chiefly concerned with pioneering work, making new contacts and converts. Actually, in July 1979, eighty-two animist families were received into the church as a result of a tour of twelve days by a group of catechists and youth leaders.

Bishop Grawng's initiative in the field of the apostolate was not confined to the decisions reached at the Myitkyina convention in 1977. Toward the end of 1978 he invited group leaders from the Movement for a Better World, in Rangoon, to come to his diocese to explain the movement to sisters in Bhamo and Myitkyina so that they might adopt it.

So convinced was the bishop of the benefits of the movement in his diocese that he led all his priest-confreres to Mandalay in January 1979, to take part in a retreat and seminar conducted there by Father Lucien Mulhern, an American Franciscan who is the regional director of the movement in South East Asia. He was accompanied by Father Theodore Nabani from Bishop Byrne's diocese in the Philippines.

During those days in Mandalay Bishop Grawng and his priests got a thorough briefing on the aim and structure of the Movement for a Better World as well as detailed instructions on the way to set it up in their parishes. On their return from Mandalay the bishop organized a retreat for his catechists and assigned two of his priests to conduct it along the lines of the one the visiting priests had given them in Mandalay. He hoped that in this way the catechists would carry the message and the movement to the communities under their care.

Bishop Grawng, with his deeply pastoral instinct, is ready to adopt any technique or method calculated to bring the good news to his widely scattered flock. He has followed up the idea of having a Kachin religious program broadcast daily from Radio Veritas, a Catholic broadcasting station set up in Manila for all South East Asia. It is financed mainly by the Vatican and by American and German bishops.

The Kachin bishop is so convinced of the importance of this project that in spite of the acute shortage of priests in his diocese, he is prepared to send one of his more talented to take charge of the studio in Manila and to prepare programs suited to the people. He feels that the temporary loss to the diocese of one priest will be more than compensated for when a religious program in Kachin will be beamed to every home in the hills and lowlands of northern Burma.

Twenty-Seven

GOOD-BYE TO BURMA

During their last years in Burma the Columbans found shortages a frustration. The scarcity of medicine caused anxiety. Each Columban remaining in Burma had been there at least thirty-two years and was feeling the effects of continuous work, old age, and sickness. Typhoid broke out among them in the summer of 1977 when a young Kachin priest, Father Peter Zau Awng, brought the bacillus to Bhamo from Rangoon. Three priests were stricken, Fathers Treanor, Foley, and Collier, and although all recovered each was weakened by the ordeal.

Although the final days were frustrating, the missionaries left without bitterness. Father Kelleher said: "My thirty-eight years in Burma have been happy ones. I was fortunate in beginning my missionary work under the care of Father Gilhodes. He taught me patience and kindness and I tried to follow in his footsteps. Those years were satisfying on a human level and much more so on a spiritual plane."

As he left for good, Father Rillstone recalled his days in Burma with satisfaction: "I arrived here at the end of 1940 and since then nearly all my life has been bound up with Kachins. Most of that time has been accompanied by wars, bloodshed, and destruction.

"First the war with Japan. Then periods of comparative calm interrupted by frequent incursions of large bands of armed deserters from the defeated Chinese army from over the border. Then the sad conflict, still going on, between Kachin nationals and the central government army. In my area alone, at least ninety percent of the villages were deliberately destroyed by fire.

"The people did not sit down and weep, but set to and rebuilt. Real starvation has faced them on many occasions. They would search the jungle for roots and leaves, which, even if they were not nutritious, were at least edible. Watching the uncomplaining acceptance of hardship and sorrow, and their unbroken will to survive, has given me an immense respect and admiration for them. I have learned much from them.

"Their confidence in the priest is absolute, no matter what his nationality. Here is an incident which I think sums it up: Shortly after the war with Japan and while there were still some European and American soldiers about the area, I was walking through one of my Kachin villages in the mountains, when a little girl from the village took me by the hand, and walked along with me. One woman, a visitor to the village, and not knowing me, or that I understood the Kachin language, said to the child: 'Aren't you afraid to go along with a foreigner?' The child's reply I will never forget: 'He is not a foreigner, he is our priest.'

"The children are the most lovable in the world. It is the children that I am going to find it hardest to part with.

"While I feel sick about leaving, I know that there are several good reasons why it might be better for the church here if we nonnationals are withdrawn. But that does not make the going away any easier. Our great comfort is to know that we are handing over the church to a Kachin bishop and Kachin priests, the kind we have prayed for. We are leaving the church in good hands."

With the consecration of Bishop Grawng in 1976 the commitment of the eleven remaining Columbans was drawing to a close. They were all anxious about the future, and, deep down in their hearts dreaded the pain of parting. They realized that a complete withdrawal by the end of that year would upset the people too much and aggravate the administrative and pastoral problems Bishop Grawng would have when all the Columbans were gone. So, they decided that a phased withdrawal over two years would be in the best interests of the diocese and its people.

They knew that Bishop Grawng would be ordaining another Kachin priest, Francis Gumbtoi, in March 1978. They also knew that Bishop Gobbato of Taunggyi had assured Bishop Grawng that he would, in 1978, give him two young priests on loan for four years. That gesture of fraternal cooperation, so much in keeping with the character of that big-hearted man, was a great boost to the morale of the new bishop and his Kachin priests at a time they needed it.

When Father Foley put the proposed phased withdrawal to the new superior general, Father Anthony O'Brien, he gave it his full approval.

The Columbans then agreed among themselves that their departure in each individual case would be conditioned by the availability of a local priest capable of taking over their respective work, pastoral or administrative.

Only six Columbans remained in the diocese at the beginning of 1978, and of these, Fathers Kelleher, O'Brien, and Treanor left in the late summer of that year. The three remaining Columbans, Fathers Foley, Cloonan, and O'Sullivan, had decided, in accordance with the terms of the amended withdrawal plan, to leave Burma later in 1978. Unfortunately this became impossible when Father Cloonan, and later Father Foley, became seriously ill. The doctors in Bhamo and Myitkyina advised Father Cloonan not to attempt a long journey by plane to Europe until the spring of 1979 at the earliest.

His two companions decided to wait for him. A further complication in Father Cloonan's health, when he arrived in Rangoon in May, delayed their final departure until July 2. It was a time of great anxiety for all three.

When the last Columbans departed Burma they left behind eight confreres: Patrick Usher, Thomas Murphy, Thomas Walsh, Thomas McEvoy, John Dunlea, Daniel McGeown, James Fitzpatrick, and John Walsh, all buried there. Two of them, Thomas Murphy and John Walsh, had died violent deaths, and in so doing, had joined nineteen other Columbans who died violently in the sixty-two years since the mission society was formed.

The old Burma hands are scattered now on new assignments throughout the world: Chicago, Perth, Navan, Liverpool, Wellington, Killiney, Birmingham, Derry, Lahinch, London, Mayo. Wherever they go they carry their memories: musical laughter down a village street at dusk; the resonant throb of temple bells; silence in a teak forest; clouds of green parrots over the river; white herons standing in a rice paddy—and, ah, the scent of jasmine.

Life is less exciting than it was, and they are homesick for Burma. As one missionary said, "The homesickness will wear away in time. Ah, yes, I'd say it will. Time heals—some."

AUTHOR'S POSTSCRIPT

While sitting in the officers' mess hall in Bhamo, in May of 1945, I saw a tall, gaunt man pause in the doorway to survey the room. His piercing eyes and quick turn of the head gave him the look of an eagle.

He wore regulation suntans, and so I took for granted he was an American officer. No insignia of rank showed on his collar, but that was not unusual; many officers had removed theirs because Japanese snipers looked for insignia in deciding where to aim.

I saw the stranger for less than five seconds, but his image stuck in my memory. Thirty years later while doing research in the archives of the Columban fathers at Killiney, in Ireland, I came upon a photograph: there he was—with the look of an eagle—Monsignor Patrick Usher.

A few minutes later I found a photograph of Father James Stuart, but that was no surprise, for I had known him in Myitkyina and Bhamo. Next I came upon a reproduction of a drawing Martha Sawyers had made just outside my door in Bhamo, a pastel portrait of Father Stuart for *Collier's* magazine. She had also done a quick pencil drawing of me and dated it May 6, 1945.

How I happened to be in Bhamo is a story that begins when Merrill's Marauders entered Burma to push the Japanese southward so that the Ledo Road could be built between India and China. At the time, I was at Fort Benning, Georgia, writing training manuals for the Infantry School.

A sign went up on the bulletin board asking for volunteers to take charge of Animal Pack Transportation Units. Mule trains. Mules were needed to carry supplies to the Marauders fighting their way through the Naga and Kachin hills.

Maybe because I had grown up on a farm in Kentucky, the army accepted my willingness to study the mystery of mules. At the Cavalry School at Fort Riley, Kansas, I joined cowboys, polo players, horse trainers, and jockeys to study spavines, saddle sores, shoeing, packing, and other matters not usual concerns of the day.

After a month of mules we started for the Far East. Three days by train from Kansas to California. Two weeks of waiting at the port of embarkation. A month by ship to Bombay. Eight days by train across India to Assam. Three days by truck down the Ledo Road.

The journey ended in a jungle near Myitkyina at dusk on Christmas Eve. As we entered a clearing we were surprised to hear Bing Crosby's voice singing *Silent Night*. The phonograph looked out of place there on the ammunition box outside a tent.

I entered the tent and handed my orders to a disheveled major who reeked of bourbon. Holding the dimly mimeographed sheet near the candle, he squinted and read with moving lips. His face went a little off center.

"Lieutenant, we don't really need you. We don't use mule trains any more. Air drop. Fly in low. Kick stuff out by parachute."

Christmas Eve on the other side of the world, and they don't need me!

Silent Night played on with a crack in it: thomp . . . thomp . . . thomp . . . thomp

There was a hint of the Columbans in the air that night, an introduction to a theme that would become a major one in my life thirty years later. For it was as a favor to a Columban that Crosby had recorded *Silent Night*. When Father Richard Ranaghan returned from Hanyang with a film of missionaries at work in China and stopped at Paramount Studios to have sound added, Bing Crosby sang *Silent Night* over a Christmas sequence: A record was pressed, and it became one of the best sellers of all time.

After that Christmas Eve, when the major had said that mule trains were no longer needed, I was assigned to serve as escort officer for fifty-seven war correspondents on the first convoy across the Ledo Road, later renamed the Stilwell Road. The 1,080-mile trip started in Ledo, Assam, followed the Ledo Road until it tied into the Burma Road, and continued on to Kunming, China. This took at least two weeks because the Japanese delayed us twice.

I flew back to Burma across the Hump to find that headquarters had moved from Myitkyina to Bhamo. There I was told to settle into a de-

serted Buddhist monastery on the Irrawaddy and write a military history telling of events in northern Burma during the past three years.

No one was long in Burma without hearing about the Columbans.

The first story I heard had to do with one of Father Stuart's practical
jokes:

An American officer, whose job it was to find out what the enemy
was up to, had told Father Stuart that he wished he could interview a
Japanese prisoner. In those days prisoners were so rare that the British
had a standing offer of a fortnight's leave to any Tommy bringing one
in.

Father Stuart said, "I know where a Japanese is, but he won't talk."

"He'll talk!" said the American. "Take me to him."

The missionary led the officer up one hill and down another and
through a couple of mountain streams. In time they reached a remote
bamboo basha. Inside was a Japanese infant.

"There, I told you he won't talk," said Father Stuart.

The afternoon that Martha Sawyers drew a portrait of Father Stuart
she wrote a letter to her editor at *Collier's.* I came upon it thirty-three
years later in the Columbian archives in Omaha:

"I had heard fabulous stories of Father Stuart for weeks at various
points throughout India and Burma, until he become a huge, tower-
ing, mythological giant shrouded in mystery. When I met him in
Bhamo to draw his portrait, I was bowled over by his personal appearance. Instead of the character I had expected, here was a short, stocky
man with a handsome Irish face which was almost too good-looking.
His voice was quiet, well modulated in tone, but he could hardly open
his mouth without saying something clever, ridiculous, or just plain
funny."

Martha Sawyers settled down to sketch Father Stuart just outside a
courtyard lined with statues of the Buddha. I sat on an ammunition
box a little to one side, not wanting to seem to be looking over her
shoulder. After a few minutes, the artist said to the missionary, "You
are a man of few words."

"Yes, but I use them over and over."

"How did you happen to become a priest?"

"The police said I could either go to jail or to the seminary."

Asked a question he could not answer, he explained, "I don't know
quite everything. You see, I was put through the seminary on an incomplete purse."

In time he warmed up enough to tell of how Merrill's Marauders had taken up a collection to finance a church in the Kachin hills. "I'm an Irishman, but I have gotten so much from Americans that I have become an American by extraction.' "

After completing the portrait, which included the dashing Gurkha hat, the artist held it toward Father Stuart. He studied it critically and mused, "No doubt I contributed to the beauty of it."

Such memories came rushing back thirty years almost to the day, when I stood at the grave of James Stuart at Navan, in Ireland. Had the situation been reversed he would have said in his soft way, "Ah, yes, he has gone to where the comfort is."

At the grave, I thought, it is a miracle that he lived for forty-six years, remembering the occasion he threw himself onto the floor of a bamboo hut just as bullets tore through the back of the cane chair on which he had been sitting, or when he flattened himself against a tree as machine-gun slugs chewed away the bark on each side.

And his many illnesses! Helen Casey, a nurse assigned to a hospital in Assam, wrote of one of them. She spoke of the time Father Stuart was admitted in the summer of 1944 with a severe attack of malaria: "There was little hope of his recovery at the time, but with his splendid cooperation and his burning desire to get back to his missions, he was soon well on the road to health."

When he went to Mandalay in 1945 to greet his newly liberated colleagues they were alarmed at his exhausted condition. It was only accidentally discovered that he had been going around for some time suffering from pneumonia. From Mandalay he went to a hospital in India. A decade later his friend Father McAlindon wrote: "The hardships of his years in the jungle had taken their full toll of Father Stuart's strength, which even a visit home in 1947 did not fully revive. When he returned to Burma it was evident he was driving himself; his old vitality was gone. He returned to Ireland in 1955 on sick leave knowing in his heart, but not admitting it, that he would never see Burma again. He died suddenly on August 11."

From time to time through the years I wondered whatever happened to my mules. A hint of the answer came in August of 1978 in the Columban archives in Omaha when a photograph turned up showing Father James Feighery riding across a stream in Burma aboard an animal that had the fine, compact conformation of an army mule. A month later I mentioned this to Father James Devine, who said, yes, it was an army mule. At the end of the war Father Devine had heard that such animals could be had for the asking, and so he sent his catechist on a two-day journey to see an American sergeant who was anxious to find good homes for the redundant mules. The Columbans can have forty, the sergeant said. The catechist thought that ten would suffice. The ten soon became missionaries when Father Devine distributed them to his confreres in the Kachin hills.

Father Devine marveled at how well-mannered those mules were. Native ponies, he said, let their eyes roll white and their nostrils flare red at any sudden sound, but the mules remained nonchalant. I explained how such manners were inculcated after the animals had arrived, green and mean, at the Cavalry School at Fort Riley. So that they would not take off at the first sound of a mortar shell we gave them a noisy schooling. Inside a stone corral some of us sat atop the mules while others threw metal helmets and firecrackers at their hooves. Paroxysms of wild-eyed fear gave way, little by little, to resigned passivity.

I forgot to ask Father Devine if he had noticed that the mules refrained from braying even when native ponies whinnied at the approach of strange animals. So that they would not give us away by reacting to the scent of their counterparts among the Japanese, a veterinarian tampered with their vocal cords.

Because I had volunteered as a muleskinner, the Columbans entered my life briefly only to drop out of it for the next thirty years. They reentered in an equally improbable way, but for a much longer duration.

This part of the story begins when I wrote a book, *Why Americans Retire Abroad*, and a student in my class at Notre Dame gave a copy to her father for Christmas. He did not read it until the following spring while on vacation in Florida, when he and his daughter decided, for some mysterious reason, that the man who wrote the book ought to write the offbeat life story of a Columban, Harold Henry.

The student's father, on his way back to Minneapolis, stopped at the Morris Inn on the Notre Dame campus and asked that I have breakfast with him. He proceeded to tell me exciting anecdotes about a Minneapolis boy who had gone to Korea forty-two years earlier and had become an archbishop there.

''Wouldn't his life make a good book?'' he asked. ''Yes.'' ''Will you write it?'' ''Yes.'' It was that sudden.

Archbishop Henry visited me briefly at Notre Dame; I stayed at his home on Cheju Island, in South Korea, for six weeks; and I saw him briefly in his native Minneapolis. The result was *Light in the Far East*.

This led to telling the story of another Columban, Archbishop Patrick Cronin. I went to the Philippines to visit him on Mindanao, and we later spent time together in his native Ireland. The result was *Mindanao Mission*.

This book is the third of a trilogy. Because of the political situation I have not returned to Burma, but I have come to know several old Burma hands: Bishop John Howe, Fathers Laurence McMahon, James Foley, James Devine, William Kehoe, Daniel Treanor, James Cloonan, Jeremiah Kelleher, Hugh O'Rourke, James McGonagle. Fortunately, of all the assignments that the United States Army could have given me during the Second World War, it sent me to two remote towns in Burma: Myitkyina and Bhamo.

Writing these three books has been a spiritual retreat. For one thing I learned that missionaries have more strength of character than I have, a greater ability to endure. They can live with dishevelment, lack of civilization, and dreariness in a way that I cannot. In coming upon a village, mangy and dismal, I knew I would soon be passing on, but a missionary knows he must work out his destiny in such places. How his soul must groan!

The research for these books was like a sermon about mortality. While reading through fifty years of *The Far East* magazine, I was reminded, time and again, of the brevity of life. Perhaps on Monday I would come across a photograph of the fresh faces of newly ordained priests; on Tuesday I would leaf past pages showing them in middle years, faces broader and bodies thicker; on Wednesday morning they might have the gray bent look of old men, and by afternoon I might turn up a picture with a black border around it. So little time.

Never have I so much enjoyed writing a book; it has been a reunion with the past. Each dawn I approached the typewriter with expectation. Why my Burma days are recalled with such affection is beyond explaining for they were difficult enough. And yet completing these pages is like saying good-bye to an old friend. It is with regret that I write the last sentence.

Edward Fischer
Notre Dame